The AND Asset

The Secret Way to Save and Use Your Money at the Same Time

Caleb Guilliams

BETTER WEALTH
PUBLISHING

Editor: Dan Kaminski
Illustrator: Becca Krahn

ISBN-13: 978-1-7327249-0-7
ISBN-10: 1-7327249-0-3

Second Print Edition
October 2018

Better Wealth Solutions
101 Division Street North
Stevens Point, Wisconsin 54481
www.betterwealthsolutions.com

Dedication

"To those who are on a journey to find a better way"

Acknowledgments

J.G. Rosholt – You're probably the only bank CEO in the country that would willingly offer a 19-year-old the keys to an entire investment department. The autonomy you allowed, empowered me to discover and implement the very best ways to serve people's financial needs. You saw a potential in me that I didn't know existed at the time. If it weren't for your leadership and support I wouldn't be where I am today.

This book and my life are simply products of the incredible people that have so willingly provided their time and knowledge to me. I want to thank my parents for their loving upbringing and always believing in me. My family and friends who have always been a huge support system. The men and women who selflessly mentored me in my fledgling years. My colleagues, who perhaps unknowingly, mentored me as I learned key concepts via text, audio and video. My clients who entrust me with their present and future livelihood. Finally, my incredible team members who make everything I do possible – I am forever grateful.

Introduction

Welcome! Allow me to ask you a fundamental question. If money wasn't an issue what would you be doing with your life? What things would you be doing if you didn't have to worry about money? More importantly, what things would you stop doing immediately if money wasn't an issue?

What I'm about to share with you in this book would be worth very little if you don't truly know "**Why**" it matters to you personally. The value of your life is not found in a hefty bank account or in being financially free. There is more to your life. It's imperative that you find your **Why**.

I often find that people discover their underlying **Why** when I ask the question – "What would you be doing if money wasn't an issue?"

You are compelled by something. You are passionate about something. Maybe it's spending quality time with family. Maybe it's travel and discovery. Maybe it's serving and alleviating need and suffering. Maybe it's starting a business that solves a significant problem or brings some valuable good or service to people. In other words, you would be living life on your terms. It's in this passion or drive that you will find your **Why**. Pondering these thoughts is what led me to write this book.

Financial independence, often referred to as financial freedom, is having enough passive income to cover your desired lifestyle. Let's assume you have achieved financial freedom, what would you do?

When it comes to money, most people are aware of what to do. It's clear that in order to get ahead financially, you need to make money, save money and have that money grow. Most people know that's what they need to do. A significantly smaller number of people are skilled in how to do those things.

Very few people have defined and embraced their **Why**. It is the **Why**, however, that makes the greatest difference.

It is knowing your **Why** that leads to success. Your life is as big as your individual **Why**.

In one sense, this book is about money. It's all about increasing your wealth by understanding how to unlock all the wealth inefficiencies you currently experience in your life. Reading this book will allow you to learn the secrets of "compound interest" and how to grow your wealth without excessive government interaction, market losses or unnecessary fees. On top of that, you will also learn the very best way to use your money throughout your life. The strategies I will show you will be invaluable whether your goal is to do some investing, start a business, pay off debt, buy a car or go on that dream vacation you have always wanted.

In another sense, this book has nothing to do with money. It has everything to do with you. Your potential, your dreams, your life. This book will lay out what I believe is the very best way for you to see and reach your highest potential by showing how to have mastery over your money. Think of this book as a guide that will allow you to start thinking about your life differently. It is my belief that many people aren't able to live the life they want because of how they think about money. I can help you end that today!

I have a simple mission statement that I want to live my life by. It reads as follows: "Help people see and reach their highest potential." My goal for this book is to help you see and reach your highest potential too.

You are your own greatest asset! Your ability to think then act is one of the greatest qualities you have as a human being. You also have another great asset that can work for you – time. Your ability to think and act in a strategic manner can lead to tremendous wealth accumulation over time.

This book is my best effort to share with you what I firmly believe is the greatest way to invest in yourself now and in the future.

When I started my journey, I had an entrepreneurial/financial planning dilemma. I knew that I was my own greatest asset. From an entrepreneurial perspective, I wanted to keep as much money as possible readily available so that I could invest in myself. However, from a financial planning perspective, I knew that if I could start saving for retirement at a young age my wealth would grow with the power of compound interest.

I believe that many people share this short-term/long-term dilemma. In this book I will walk you through the best ways to live well in the present while still planning for the future.

There are a lot of books out there that purport to help people to live the life they want to live.

What separates this book from all the others is that I don't focus on WHAT you do. Rather, I show you radically better ways HOW to do what you're currently doing.

One thing that I hope you can agree with me on is the value of time. This book will show you better ways to buy back your time so that you can do the things that you absolutely love.

Which of these apply to you?

Entrepreneur – This book will show you better ways to use your money in your business or entrepreneurial endeavors.

Investor – Real estate, stocks, bonds, options, crypto currency, etc. This book will show you a better way to invest.

High Income – Pay a lot in taxes, can't contribute to a Roth IRA. This book will show you a better way to save more money and leverage your assets.

Inexperienced – You might have just started thinking about saving and investing. This book will open your eyes to the possibilities of how to master money management.

Experienced – You might be an experienced investor and have done very well with your money. This book will help you learn ways to enhance your wealth success.

Retirement – Near retirement or already retired. This book will show you better ways to increase your wealth and preserve it.

Family – Planning your next vacation or how to fund college. This book will show you a better way to save for the future while also getting to live well in the present with your family.

Debt – Looking for ways to reduce or eliminate debt? This book will show you how to save more money and pay off debt at the same time.

Before you start reading I encourage you to really think about the question I asked earlier – "If money wasn't an issue what would you be doing with your life?" Also, consider what is your **Why**?

Feel free to write down your answers below:

This book Is divided into three sections:

Section 1 – The Wealth Equation

In this section I will explain the following concepts:

The Wealth Equation – You will learn why I think this equation is a powerful way to describe the best financial strategy available today.

Efficiency – You will look at areas where you may be struggling, (perhaps without realizing it), with inefficiencies. You will also explore the most efficient way to compare various places to invest money.

Section 2 – Compounding And Control

In this section, I will explain two additional important concepts:

Compounding – You will explore in detail the power of compounding growth. Very few people are taking full advantage of this powerful wealth building tool. You will learn how different kinds of interest can be used to your advantage.

Control – You will look at the positive effects of having control over your money. I believe being able to control money in the short-term as well as long-term is a critical yet severely underutilized tool in most financial plans and strategies.

With an understanding of the power of Efficiency, Compounding and Control I will explain how you can save money and get true compounding growth while also being in full control of this money and corresponding wealth accumulation.

Section 3 – The Controlled Compounding Strategy™

In this section, I am going to lay out what I believe is one of the most powerful wealth strategies that will put you on a journey to financial security and independence. I am first going to look at why and how this strategy works.

We are going to discover the most ideal place for you to save your money. Then, if I did my job correctly, you will know how you can have total control over your money today and in the future while also letting it grow with uninterrupted compounding.

There may be better strategies or other ideal accounts in the future. But, at the time of writing this book, I am giving you what I believe is the very best way to save and use money throughout your life.

Whether you're in debt with a negative net worth or own a billion dollar business, in some way, you can apply the principles of this strategy in your own life. This strategy won't replace what you're currently doing, but it will, hopefully, show you a better way how to do what you're doing.

Please allow me a friendly suggestion. While it may be tempting to immediately jump to Section 3, I would really encourage you to read this book in its entirety. Strategies can come and go, but the principles within this book are universal.

Contents

Section 1
The Wealth Equation

1

Financial Freedom – What is it and How Do You Obtain it?

Financial freedom is something that is very specific to you. You are financially dependent as long as the money you need to generate is dependent on you working for it. You become financially independent, or financially free, when you no longer have to work in order for all of your expenses to be covered by your income.

That is a basic working definition of financial freedom, but your life is much bigger than expenses and income.

The good news is that financial freedom is attainable – if you take the right steps. Remember, you are your greatest asset.

Your ability to create value (income) and your continual value (potential future income) is your greatest asset.

When planning, many typical financial advisors solely look at your saved assets and ask the question: "How can you get a good rate of return from your assets?" Unfortunately, this is a terribly small-minded and short-sighted approach. You don't maximize the value of your life by just utilizing your present savings.

Instead, I suggest you use your resources, particularly money and time, in order to have the greatest impact on your life. When it comes to your financial future, have your goals in mind, and make decisions based on maximizing your financial potential.

This way, you will attain financial independence when your sustainable passive income (money that you don't have to work for) is sufficient enough to finance your Why.

Financial independence is definitely attainable. Whatever your age and stage in life, you can make solid progress toward building a passive income stream that will finance your life and your **Why** at a level beyond what you currently may think is possible.

Want to know how?

Introducing... The Most Famous Equation

The most famous equation in the world was derived by Albert Einstein in 1905. It is instantly recognizable but not always understood by people. The effects of this equation are colossal!

The equation explains how the sun and stars work by using nuclear fusion. It made nuclear power plants and the atomic bomb possible by explaining the energy produced by one and released by the other. It made medical radiology feasible. Applications as diverse as carbon-dating, topography scanning and telecommunication satellites owe their existence to this equation. It would be difficult to overstate the powerful impact of this equation on our world today.

As you may have guessed, that most famous equation is $E=mc^2$. What you may not know is that Einstein formulated this equation as a young man before he had obtained his doctorate in physics, a teaching position and access to research facilities or funding. At the age of 26, he formulated this equation by wrestling with three fundamental problems in physics that had not been addressed. After producing four papers on the subject, he submitted them for publication in the German "Journal of Physics." The last of these four papers contained the equation $E=mc^2$.

While Einstein was delighted to have his work published, the significance of his equation was not immediately grasped or universally accepted. Despite these humble beginnings, the equation has proven its truthfulness and value.

The principles behind it are rock solid, and the ramifications of it in the real world of practical experience (not just the world of theory and ideology) are firmly established. In fact, anyone setting out into the realm of science would be wise to chart a course on the path created and governed by the principles embodied in $E=mc^2$.

Situations similar to Einstein's also occur in the financial world. I've spent years learning about reliable principles and truths relative to finances that would help my clients. Then, I learned how to effectively communicate these principles and truths in ways that could be acted upon decisively by my clients.

The Wealth Equation:

The wealth equation states that maximum efficiency is achieved by multiplying your money through the processes of uninterrupted compounding and unhindered control.

Maximum Efficiency = money (uninterrupted compounding x unhindered control)

...which can also be written as

Efficiency = money (compounded x controlled)

...or

E=m (c x c)

...and finally,

E=mc²

Like Einstein's equation, you may not initially understand it when you see it. But, I'm confident that it will prove its truth and value in your personal finances!

2

Efficiency

Let's look at the importance of efficiency, or the "E" in $E=mc^2$. We'll call this the "Big E" because maximizing efficiency involves the whole process of growth, income and legacy. It's all about getting your money to work for you more and more as the years go by.

The wealth equation ($E=mc^2$) is a deceptively simple, immensely powerful and astonishingly effective formula that can help anyone achieve financial independence so let's break it down in simple terms and put it to work. To start, let's talk about efficiency.

Financial Freedom Begins With Efficiency

If you were to only get one thing out of this book, I hope it's the concept of efficiency. Whatever dreams you have, and whatever path you take to accomplish those dreams, I hope the information in this book inspires and equips you to pursue the most efficient financial path toward that end, because the better way is the most efficient way.

To illustrate this example of efficiency, let's look at an example from the game of golf.

Club vs. Swing

If you wanted to excel at golf and could choose to have the very best club on the market or the swing of your favorite professional golfer, which would you choose?

Most people with knowledge of the game would choose the swing in a heartbeat because perfecting your swing is far more valuable than having the very best club. It literally separates the best golfers from everyone else!

The financial services industry is made up of many individuals selling products rather than teaching the process. It's similar to giving someone the very best golf club and expecting them to be a great golfer even though they have never practiced their swing.

Unfortunately, this is the reality that faces so many trying to get ahead financially.

Rather than focusing on a product, (buying a better club) the better way is to focus on the process (developing your swing) of building wealth. This process starts with understanding wealth transfers and the opportunity cost (which I will explain later in the book), that comes from losing money unknowingly and unnecessarily.

Since efficiency matters, the conversation must begin by focusing on the process before the product. In this chapter, I hope to share with you some powerful principles that will allow you to master the process of efficiency in your own life. I will also share with you the 16 characteristics of what would be an ideal financial vehicle (club) to use when deciding where to save or invest your money.

The Swing – The Process

When you shop for a car, you'll see gas mileage numbers that represents the mileage you will get if you drive in the city and the mileage you get when you drive longer distances on the highway. Highway mileage is always going to be a higher number than city mileage because of efficiency.

When you drive a long distance on the highway, you use a significant amount of fuel to get up to speed. But once you get up to cruising speed, it takes much less fuel to maintain that speed. Generally, in the city you are starting and stopping frequently. This is what lowers the number for city mileage.

Being efficient with your money (by minimizing losses, maximizing gains and mastering control) is like getting highway mileage in your vehicle. It takes a bit to get up to speed. But, if you can avoid starting and stopping and allow efficiencies to do the work, you will get much further much faster.

That's why I stress a specific strategy that focuses on managing your money with maximum efficiency.

Whatever your current financial plan is, you are likely losing money unknowingly or unnecessarily. Finding those losses and putting an end to them is crucial to maximizing the efficiency of your wealth plan.

Warren Buffett is widely considered one of the most successful investors in the world. He is a frugal saver who has launched innumerable entrepreneurial ventures and has pledged to give away 99% of his wealth. He has two rules to investing:

1. **Don't lose money!**
2. **Listen to rule number one!**

Warren Buffett is more concerned with preventing losses than he is with making great gains. There is a good reason for that; losses affect your money more than gains. When you lose money, you're losing your future earning potential.

The term I use for a loss is a "wealth transfer." Any time you lose money, your wealth is leaving you and being transferred to someone else. I picked up the term "wealth transfer" from Don Blanton in his book *Your Circle of Wealth* and I use it regularly with clients. Wealth transfers can occur any time you make a financial decision regardless of your situation.

The significant financial expenses you have may include buying homes, paying taxes, fees, education, investing and major purchases (like vacations, cars, etc.). Wealth transfers can happen during any of these transactions and can happen without you knowing. Any time a wealth transfer occurs, you lose more than you think.

What's the true cost of a wealth transfer? Well, it's significantly more than just the initial loss. When you lose a dollar, you don't just lose that dollar, but you also lose the opportunity of what that dollar could have earned you over time. A question that should be asked is: "What would a wealth transfer be worth if it was kept and allowed to grow?"

That amount is called an "opportunity cost" and is a fundamental truth about money. The basic definition of opportunity cost is the loss of potential gain from other alternatives when one alternative is chosen. All of your decisions have secondary effects, either positive or negative.

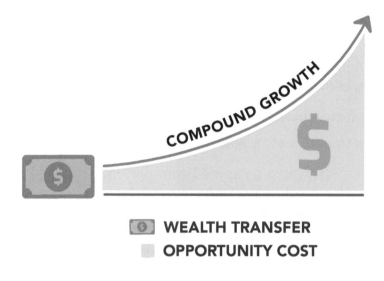

WEALTH TRANSFER
OPPORTUNITY COST

Once you grasp the concept of opportunity cost, you will view the world and money differently. Ultimately, it's having the understanding that your decisions have consequences. For example, you may start to realize the true cost of a four dollar latte (what could those four dollars be worth in the future?). Opportunity cost can be very empowering because you have something solid to work with. You can determine the true cost of not investing in something or investing in yourself.

A good example of investing in yourself is starting a business. The initial cost for me to start my financial business took a significant part of my time and money. However, the decision offered many benefits, and ultimately, was something I had to do in order to help as many people see and reach their highest potential.

My suggestion is to never make a decision based solely off of numbers. Rather, look at how that decision will help you get closer to or farther from your underlying **Why.**

Opportunity costs, like a four dollar latte, may not be terribly impressive. Just imagine adding a few zeros to that number. What if I could show you how to prevent $4,000 or even $40,000 in losses? What about preventing $400,000, $4 million, or even more in losses?

How could that affect your net worth? How could it affect your earnings potential? And perhaps most importantly—if I could show you how to prevent losing a significant amount of money, would you then turn around and invest that money in the most efficient way possible?

Wealth transfers affect your net worth far more than gains do because when you lose money, you have less capital working for you, meaning less opportunity to make gains.

Since wealth transfers are so important to maximizing the overall efficiency of your financial plan, let's look at some of them in a little more detail. There are four main types of wealth transfers that are working against your money: investment loss, taxes, fees and what I'm going to call *use.*

Wealth Transfers Due to Investment Loss

Risk is the chance that you will lose money. Only in financial planning do people say things like "higher risk = higher return." What that really means is that you'll have a greater chance of making money if you do something that has a greater chance of losing money. In what world does that type of logic make sense? In reality, as you will see, you can't afford to lose money at any time, no matter your age or risk tolerance.

One of the wealth transfers you are likely experiencing is investment loss. Many people believe they are saving for retirement but the reality is they are investing. What's the difference?

Money you invest is money that is subject to loss. Whereas, your savings consist of money that you can't lose. This is another truth about money which has been blurred by those in the financial services industry.

Money that you are saving is, by definition, money that you are keeping safe. For many people, that means that it's unproductive, just stuffed into a mattress or a savings account that earns next to nothing. Saving does not have to be that way. Just because your money is safe doesn't mean it can't grow.

In fact, by the time you finish this book, you'll know how to enable your savings to outperform the most common investments available today.

Money that is saved doesn't have to be unproductive. It should be safe and not subject to loss. A majority of people are encouraged to *save* for retirement through the *use* of mutual funds. However, mutual funds are an investment product. They are not a savings product because any money in the stock market is subject to risk. Many individuals are storing most, if not all of their retirement money in financial vehicles that are subject to loss. As history has shown, a single event can cause significant value loss within a matter of a few days!

Additionally, if you are involved in any investment that includes stocks, bonds or mutual funds, you are losing more money than you think you are. This is because of the difference between average and actual rate of return (ROR). The average ROR you are shown on your account statement is almost always going to be higher than the actual ROR you are getting on your investment. Let me show you a quick example of why this is true.

Average vs. Actual

Let's say you have $100 to invest in a mutual fund. The first year, that fund grows by 100% which leaves you with an account value of $200. The second year, your fund unfortunately decreases by 50%, diminishing your account value back to your original $100. Wall Street says you're an incredible investor because you've earned an average ROR of 25%! However, since your account balance is back to the original contribution, your actual ROR is 0%.

As you will discover, your actual ROR is in fact negative if you include taxes, fees and inflation.

INITIAL BALANCE: **$100**

YEAR	ANNUAL RETURN	ANNUAL GAIN/(LOSS)	END OF YEAR BALANCE
1	+100%	$100	$200
2	-50%	($100)	$100

AVERAGE RETURN: 25%	ACTUAL RETURN: 0%

Here is the money truth! Any computation of average ROR is going to under represent losses and over represent gains, unless you add money to the investment. It's just how the math works. Losses are always greater because you are losing from a larger number. Gains are always smaller because you are gaining on a smaller number. Most people are unknowingly and unnecessarily transferring wealth away from themselves through market losses.

And remember, the loss of a dollar to market loss is compounded by the fact that you are not just losing that dollar but you are also losing what that dollar could earn you well into the future.

Wealth Transfers Due to Tax Loss

In 1913 a tax was proposed and described as "temporary." It was never to exceed 7% of income. This tax has continued to this day, and is now known as the "Federal Income Tax." For some, taxes could end up being the biggest wealth eroder. This could be a huge wealth transfer. It all depends on how and when taxes are paid.

While many individuals often focus on the tax rate, another area that may fluctuate is the threshold of the tax brackets. This threshold can change from one year to the next and cause an unexpected wealth transfer.

Are taxes going up or going down? No one can be certain of the answer to this, but at the time of the writing of this book, the U.S. Government passed a large (temporary for many individuals) tax cut. When taxes are historically high, it might be reasonable to expect them to fall, but since taxes are currently historically low, it's reasonable to expect them to rise. While no one can be certain, it is likely that taxes aren't going down any further and could very easily go up in the future.

It is vital that your money grows efficiently while considering the changing tax environment.

Minimizing wealth transfers that are a result of taxation starts with getting a firm grasp on three types of financial accounts that are available to you; taxable, tax-deferred and tax-free.

Here is a quick overview of the differences:

Taxable Accounts use after-tax dollars. You have already paid income tax on the money you put into these accounts. Those dollars then grow in a taxable environment so that if you sell that investment or receive income from it, you either have to pay additional income tax or capital gains tax. There are no penalties involved in accessing your money in a taxable account. You are free to leave it in the account as long as you'd like and you're free to take it out whenever you wish. The effect of using a taxable account is that you are only taxed on your gains, not the initial principal. A taxable account does little to minimize wealth transfers due to taxes.

Tax-deferred Accounts use pre-tax dollars. You are deferring, postponing or putting off paying taxes on these dollars. Your account then grows in a tax-deferred environment. Unlike taxable and tax-free accounts, in most cases, you will pay a penalty if you access your money early. You are also obligated to begin to take your money out at a certain point later in life. When taking money out of the account, the principal you put in and the gains you received are taxed as income. None of the gains are taxed at a capital gains rate, which is most often lower.

A tax-deferred account has the most restrictions. It postpones the whole tax bill to the future, and you give up total control of how efficient you can be. The only way this account is more efficient in the long run relative to taxes, is if you are in a lower tax bracket when you begin to withdraw money.

For these reasons, I believe a tax-deferred account is the least effective at minimizing wealth transfers when it comes to taxes.

Yes, you read that right! To most people, the great appeal of these accounts is the short-term benefit of not paying taxes on the principal or the gain. Little thought is given to the risk of "kicking the can" down the road and paying taxes at a later date. In exchange for the opportunity to defer payment of taxes, you give up a certain level of control. As you'll see when I expand upon the wealth equation, maintaining control is indispensable.

Many people invest most of their entire financial future in these types of plans without really understanding the consequences. These plans are sold as "tax sheltered" plans because they offer people a way to utilize pre-tax dollars and have their money grow tax-deferred. That's what makes them so attractive today. What many people forget is your money is locked up and can't be accessed without a penalty. You will also have to pay taxes on all of your money in the future at an unknown tax rate.

Here's another way to think about it. You walk into a bank to get a loan. The bank approves you for the loan and you are thrilled. Before receiving the money, you want to know two things — when you have to pay the money back and what the interest rate is. The bank tells you that you can pay them back in 30 years, and when you do, they'll look at what they need at that time and then tell you the interest rate. There is no way you would take this deal! Yet, this is exactly the kind of offer you might be utilizing with a tax-deferred plan.

Tax-free Accounts use after-tax dollars. You have already paid income tax on the money you put into these types of accounts. However, unlike a taxable account, these dollars grow in a tax-free environment. You do not pay taxes on your gains. And, in most cases, you can access your money tax-free. It's your money to do with as you please.

A tax-free account is, in most cases, the most effective at minimizing wealth transfers due to taxes.

Keep in mind that, ultimately, the loss of a dollar to taxes is compounded by the fact that you are not just losing that dollar, but, you are also losing what that dollar could have earned for the rest of your life. The opportunity cost of wealth transfers due to taxes now and in the future can be staggering. Later in this book, I will share much more scary thoughts about why I believe taxes are going to go up, and I mean way up.

Wealth Transfers Due to Fees

A third type of wealth transfer that you want to minimize in order to be the most efficient in your financial plan relates to fees. Fees can be deceptively damaging because they are usually somewhat hidden and advertised as being low. Think of fees as a silent tax on your wealth potential. Fees may look small, and it can be difficult to see that they present a real threat to your wealth. Let me show you three examples of how much money you may be losing in fees.

Percentage

One way to envision losses due to fees is to think in terms of percentages. If you make a 4% gain on your investment but lose 2% of that gain to fees, you have actually only made a 2% gain.

If you make an 8% gain on your investment but lose 2% of that gain to fees, you have actually only made a 6% gain. Looking at it this way, you can see that even with a low fee, you lose anywhere from 25%-50% of your growth to fees.

Time to Double

A second way to get an idea of the effect of fees is to think in terms of how long it takes to double your money. If you are getting a 4% return, your money will double in 18 years. If there's a 2% fee involved, it will take 37 years to double. If you are fortunate enough to get an 8% return, your money will double in nine years, but if you are paying a 2% fee it will take you 13 years.

4% TIME TO DOUBLE

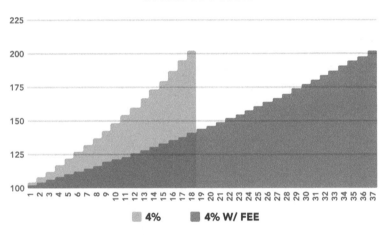

8% TIME TO DOUBLE

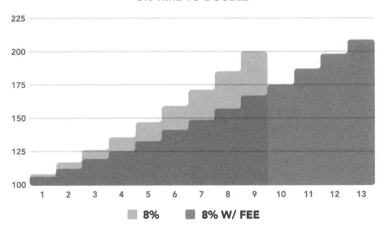

When you look at it this way, you can begin to understand how seemingly small fees can hinder your ability to multiply your money.

Actual Value

A third way to understand the real cost of fees is to use actual numbers. If you contributed $10,000 every year to an account that earned 4%, you would have an account balance of $583,283 after 30 years. With a 2% fee, your account value would drop to $416,662. That's a difference of $166,621! You personally would have paid $109,023 in fees; the rest was lost due to opportunity cost.

If instead you were able to earn an 8% ROR without fees, your account balance would be $1,223,459. With a 2% fee, your account value would drop to $830,162. That's a difference of $393,297! In this example, you personally would have paid $173,343 in fees, and a sizeable $219,954 was lost due to opportunity cost.

In all of these examples, you assume you don't lose any money in the investment itself. In most situations you have to pay fees whether you make money or not!

ACTUAL VALUE

Wealth Transfers Due To Use

The concept of wealth transfers due to *use* is very important to understand. This is by far the most powerful wealth transfer.

Understanding why it's so powerful can truly be a game changer. Instead of it working against you, you will learn how to get it to work for you.

When I ask people what their greatest financial need is, they usually think it is saving money for retirement or other major life needs. I disagree. I think your greatest financial need is spending money wisely. You spend or *use* way more money than you save or invest. If you were more efficient with the money that you *use*, it could make a massive difference to your bottom line.

Whenever you buy something, you are either paying interest or losing the ability to earn interest. Let me give you an example.

I drove my dad's car (a late 90's Geo Prizm) around all through high school, and though it didn't have air conditioning and wasn't much to look at, I have really fond memories of it. I passed it down to my younger brother when I bought my first car, a 2011 Ford Fusion.

I was really happy because I initially thought I had gotten a really great deal. It was more than a step up from the Prizm I was previously driving. With leather heated seats and other niceties, it was a leap into luxury, and I paid cash for it.

When I bought it, I was pretty proud of myself because I wasn't going to be paying interest on a loan. At the time, I thought that paying cash for major purchases was the very best way to go. It had to be better than buying it on credit and paying interest, right? Not necessarily.

In a later chapter on compounding, I am going to share with you an amazing discovery I had. Using my personal car as an example, I will show you the best way to buy big ticket items.

The Club – Ideal Account

Let's step into a perfect financial world for a moment where everything works in your favor and you can make the most money with the least amount of effort.

If you could find this "ideal" environment for your money, what would it look like? In one sentence, I'd say it's an environment that compounds and controls funds in the most efficient way possible. That's a really condensed statement so let's explore the elements that would enable it to happen.

The 16 Characteristics of the Ideal Financial Vehicle Include:

1. Safe – Your money suffers no losses.

2. Liquid – Your money is accessible either for emergencies or for opportunities.

3. Growth – Your money multiplies.

4. Leverage – You can use your money as collateral.

5. Inflation-Protection – Your money grows at a rate greater than the rate of inflation.

6. Guarantees – There are contractual assurances in place.

7. Free of Fees – You do not have to pay anything to anyone for the use of the vehicle.

8. Free of Regulation – Your money is not restricted in any way.

9. Flexible – You can fund the account in whatever way works best for you.

10. Requires Minimal Time – The vehicle works on auto-pilot.

11. Passive Cash Flow – Your money produces income on its own.

12. Private – Your money grows without restrictions and has creditor protections.

13. Protection – It provides for you in the event of tragedy.

14. Tax-deductible – You can subtract any money you put into the account from your taxable income.

15. Tax-free Growth – Your money grows without being taxed.

16. Tax-free Distribution – You can access your money without paying taxes on it.

There is no vehicle that includes all of these characteristics. However, it gives you something to shoot for in your journey to financial freedom. More than that, it gives you the right thing to shoot for.

It's not enough to just compare financial vehicles, options and opportunities to each other. You need to compare everything to the ideal. After all, you want maximum efficiency on everything included in the list above.

Later in the book, I'll share a financial vehicle which comes as close to the ideal as possible. I call it the "Master Account." For now, just know that when I talk about a Master Account, I'm referring to a financial vehicle that has the greatest number of the ideal characteristics mentioned above.

Maximize

In the process of writing this book and meeting with prospective clients, I found myself using the word "maximize" a lot. I mean, a lot. I used it so often that it was sort of embarrassing. I sounded like a broken record. That's when I started searching for synonyms.

Surprisingly, it turns out that there are no other words I can use to get across the same idea! Sure, I found "amplify," "expand," "stretch," and plenty of other words that convey the idea of "getting larger." But, when I use the term, "maximize," I mean amplifying, expanding or stretching to the greatest extent possible.

Your best path toward financing your life and your **Why** is to "maximize the efficiency of your money." Don't just amplify, expand or stretch it. Instead, go to the greatest extent possible to get as close to the ideal as possible. This challenges a lot of conventional wisdom. Let me offer another example.

Foot Off the Brake

In this chapter, I made a reference stating that highway mileage is better than city mileage because of efficiency. Financially, when someone is at maximum efficiency, they are not incurring any unnecessary losses, and they are achieving the most compounding of interest and control possible. They are cruising down the highway toward their chosen destination with minimum effort and maximum speed.

When someone is being inefficient financially, they are allowing unnecessary wealth transfers and putting their money in places where they have little control. It is as if they have one foot on the gas pedal and the other firmly pressing down on the brake.

Many people are trying to get to somewhere by pressing harder and harder on the gas pedal (working more hours, looking for a better ROR, taking greater risks, etc.). They are unaware that they are also stepping on the brake (paying too much in fees, losing earning potential to taxes, missing opportunities due to lack of capital, etc.).

Efficiency is about ensuring that the whole car (the whole system and strategy you are counting on to get you to your **Why**) is functioning at its peak capacity. This means no wasted energy and no unnecessary drag.

Efficiency (the E in $E=mc^2$) will only make whatever you are doing better. It will make it better through all the stages of your life. Whether you are an entrepreneur, an investor, an employee or a retiree, maximizing the efficiency of your financial strategy from beginning to end is sure to enhance whatever you are doing.

To evaluate a real-world practical example of efficiency, let's explore what many people consider to be their primary investment – their home.

3

Most Efficient Way to Buy a House

I'm not going to go into a philosophical discussion of owning versus renting a house. I won't try to convince you that you can save more money if you downsize. I'm simply going to analyze what is the most efficient way to buy a house. Why?

Most people are more emotionally invested in this financial decision than any other one that they make. After all, it's their home and not just a house. It's a place where they can relax and feel comfortable being themselves every day, raise their family, celebrate holidays and special occasions, take part in hobbies, entertain and more.

However, there are some important things to consider with this big purchase; how you pay for your house matters.

When it comes to efficiently buying a house, you need to look at three areas:

1. How to minimize loss (wealth transfers).

2. How to maximize future growth (opportunity cost).

3. How to have the most security (control).

The issues involved in buying a house are essentially between how you pay for it and when you pay it off.

With regards to how you pay for it, there are two basic options; you can pay with cash or finance it. With regards to when you pay it off, there are many different strategies so you will need to explore both ends of the spectrum. You can either pay it off as quickly as possible or pay it off over as long a time as possible.

Keep in mind that you are looking for the most efficient solution. That may or may not be the most comfortable or commonly used solution.

For this exercise, let's make four assumptions:

1. The price of the house is $250,000.

2. You have $250,000 in cash available.

3. You can get a 30 year loan at 4% interest.

4. You can access an investment that will give you a 4% return on your money for 30 years.

You have two options:

Option One: Pay Cash

Let's say you pay $250,000 in cash for the house. Then, you take the monthly payment you were going to pay the bank ($1,189) and invest it, earning a steady 4% over 30 years. This way, you end up with $828,374 in cash and a paid off house.

Option Two: Finance the House

If you finance the house at 4% and save your $250,000 in an account that earned 4%, after 30 years, you would also have $828,374 in cash and a paid-off house.

Mathematically, the results are the same, but this practically never happens because it requires the buyer to stay in the house for 30 years. It also requires the cash buyer to pay themselves faithfully for 30 years, which is also unlikely.

Now, let's discuss the most efficient way to purchase a house. With the focus on efficiency, you are going to look at several factors that interact with each other. None of them, in and of themselves, necessarily make the decision for you. But, each of them contribute important information that will help you form your decision.

Payments

Most people end up doing whatever it takes to make mortgage payments. The nature of financing is that you are obligated to pay that money back. The same is not true for savings. If you pay cash for your house, there are no payments required of you. In this example, you would need to save $1,189 every month for 30 years to pay yourself back. That's a total of $428,040.

If you paid cash for a house, how likely would you be to pay back the entire amount to yourself? In which situation are you more likely to exercise the discipline necessary to make the numbers work?

The concept of *efficiency* as used in this book doesn't tell you the answer to this one. It's something you've got to answer for yourself.

Tax Benefits

There can be some very beneficial tax advantages to a mortgage. For some, these could be the only benefits they will receive. Efficiency demands that you quantify and weigh the potential tax benefits of financing. Tax law can change so it's not an exact science, but you can make a reasonable assumption concerning the money you could save in taxes over those 30 years.

There are no tax benefits if you pay cash for your house. Efficiency comes down solidly on the side of financing in this case.

House Value

The value of your house may increase or decrease over time. One reason people choose to purchase versus rent is the chance to build equity in a property. But, as many experienced in 2008, houses can sharply fall in value unexpectedly.

What ROR does the equity in your house earn? Regardless of how it's paid for, your house will increase or decrease in value. A benefit of paying cash is not having to pay interest to a financial institution.

However, a cash buyer is going to lock up a large portion of their capital and/or net worth in their house. Meanwhile, the person that finances has that same house. But, instead of locking up their money, they can let it grow and use it for other activities. How you pay for a house is unrelated to its value. With regards to house value, efficiency is solidly on the side of financing.

Financing allows you to own an asset and have access to your funds for other investing or saving.

Inflation

Inflation is the force that makes your dollar less valuable over time. Your dollar today is as valuable as it will ever be because of inflation. If you acquired a 30 year mortgage as shown previously, your payment would be $1,189. Using a 2% inflation rate, in 15 years, that $1,189 payment would have the buying power of $883. In 30 years, that $1,189 mortgage payment would only have the buying power of $656.

A long-term fixed mortgage can be a fantastic hedge against inflation.

You can use dollars today and pay the loan back with dollars that will be worth substantially less in the future. Efficiency loves these kinds of situations.

Earning Interest vs. Paying Interest

In our example, the interest you would pay the bank on a $250,000 loan over 30 years at 4% is $178,040. The interest you would be paid if you invested your $250,000 for 30 years at 4% is $578,374. Is it a good use of your money to spend $178,040 in order to earn $578,374? Efficiency says "Yes."

Based on the spread between what you pay in interest and what you make in interest, financing the home is the more efficient (and therefore, the more profitable) decision.

COMPOUNDING INTEREST OVER 30 YEARS

INITIAL BALANCE	INTEREST RATE	MONTHLY COST	INTEREST EARNED	FINAL BALANCE
$250,000	4%	$0	$578,374	$828,374

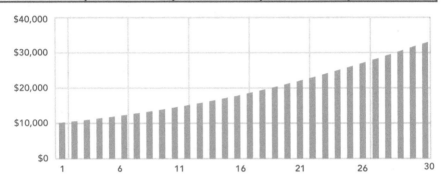

AMORTIZING INTEREST OVER 30 YEARS

INITIAL BALANCE	INTEREST RATE	MONTHLY COST	INTEREST PAID	FINAL BALANCE
$250,000	4%	$1,189	$178,040	$0

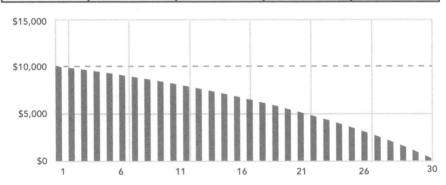

Opportunity Cost

If you pay cash for a house in this example, you tie up those funds for 30 years. However, if you finance the house, you have the $250,000 available for any opportunities you can find or create. Just because you can invest your money in something for 30 years and earn 4%, doesn't mean you have to!

Do you think that in the next 30 years, with a little help and direction, you would be likely to find a way to earn more than 4%?

In this example, you gain more control over your money and can generate greater returns by financing instead of paying cash. Yet again, efficiency suggests to finance.

Security

Many people believe that paying off their house as soon as possible is a sound, financial decision. I use the word "believe" intentionally. It's not strong enough to say that people think they should pay off their house early or that people are under that impression. For lots of people, it's a firmly held belief.

If you are one of those people, please hear me out before you toss my book in the trash. It appears to me that there are two reasons many people feel this way.

The first is that you are human and are prone to insecurity. You feel safer when you think you're in control when things are settled. Something unresolved, like a mortgage, lurks threateningly in the back of your mind.

Prone to worry, you may fret over what you would do if "something happened." You don't really think it through, strategize or make a plan for that eventuality. You just comfort yourself with thinking that if you could get the house paid off, you would at least have a place to live. I get that. I really do. The feeling of safety (that you are doing what you can to ensure your security) whether it is warranted or not, is a powerful influence.

There is a second reason many people believe so strongly in paying off their house quickly. That's what they've been taught by people whom they respect and trust. The idea that debt in any form is damaging and that you should get out of all debt as quickly as possible is a mantra of many qualified financial gurus out there.

If you pay for your house in cash, I'd argue that you are putting yourself in a less secure position. If a real crisis came along, all of your money would be tied up in your house. You would have to sell or refinance the house in order to get access to your funds and address the crisis.

Think about it in real-life terms. The crisis you are most likely to encounter may include: loss of employment, unexpected physical disability and/or economic uncertainty. Let's play out a scenario using the example above.

If a crisis were to occur, which would be the safer situation to be in:

1. Having a house to live in, but without any money?

2. Or, would you be more secure if you had $250,000 on hand with which you could manage both the payments on your house and whatever the crisis demanded?

Efficiency indicates that you are significantly safer (whether you feel that way or not) financing your home than you would be by paying cash.

By financing, you gain control of your house while only putting in a fraction of your money. The rest of your money could be multiplying in a more liquid vehicle and could quickly come to your rescue if your safety is threatened.

How you pay for your house is a big financial and emotional decision. Taking a sober look at the numbers and understanding the various issues involved can help you make a better decision.

What I've just done is shown you efficiency at work. For many people, their focus in buying a house is really narrow. They are primarily concerned with what rate they are paying or what their monthly payment will be.

It's only if you bring efficiency to the table and start asking questions and running numbers in multiple areas, that you begin to see there is so much more going on than interest rates and monthly payments.

You begin to see the whole picture. You begin to see losses you can avoid and gains you can capture. You begin to see ways that you can exercise control over the process to work it to your advantage.

If you make a number of moves to increase the efficiency of each part of the process, the whole process ends up working efficiently, and that makes a substantial difference at the end of the day. I wanted to show you the most efficient way to buy a house to illustrate the principle that it is not just what you buy, but how you buy it that matters.

Section 2
Compounding And Control

4

Uninterrupted Compounding

I've established that being efficient with your money (minimizing losses, maximizing gains and mastering control) is what will enable you to reach financial independence in the quickest and safest way possible.

If I take the wealth equation ($E=mc^2$) and put it in sentence form, it reads like this: Efficiency is multiplying your money by the use of compounding and control. In this chapter, I discuss the first "c" in the wealth equation—compounding. When used in the wealth equation, I mean a very specific type of compounding, uninterrupted compounding.

The Power of Compounding

When you invest, your money earns interest (dividends or capital gains, etc.). Interest begins to grow from the first year. However, in the second year you earn interest on your original money and the interest from the first year.

In the third year, you earn interest on your original money and the interest from the first two years. And so on. Every year you are not just earning a return, you are earning a greater return. This is compounding.

Compounding produces a return that is not just incremental, it is exponential.

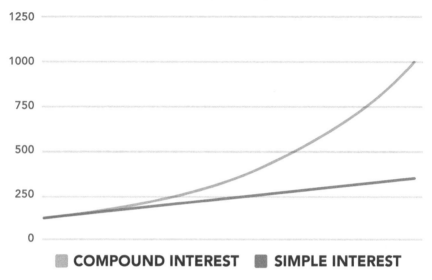

COMPOUND INTEREST ■ SIMPLE INTEREST

The Eighth Wonder of The World

Consider this choice between two options. If you were given the choice between receiving a million dollars today or receiving one penny every day doubled for 30 days, which would you choose?

If you understand the principle of compounding (and have a minute or two to do some quick calculations), you would confidently choose the penny doubled every day for the 30 day period and walk away with over five million dollars.

It is true that it takes some time for compounding to accelerate. At the end of the first week of doubling, you have only accumulated $0.64. At the end of the second week, you only see $81.92 sitting there. In fact, it takes all of 28 days before you break a million dollars. But if you stick to your guns and wait just two more days, you end up with over five million dollars!

.01	.02	.04	.08	.16	.32
.64	1.28	2.56	5.12	10.24	20.48
40.96	81.92	163.84	327.68	655.36	1,310.72
2,621.44	5,242.88	10,485.76	20,971.52	41,943.04	83,886.08
167,772.16	335,544.32	671,088.64	1,342,177.28	2,684,354.56	5,368,709.12

This is the power of compounding.

Compounding, if left alone to work its magic over time, will always produce an exponential yield. Albert Einstein has been credited over the years in various financial publications as stating: "Compound interest is the eighth wonder of the world." Another statement often attributed to him declares: "He who understands it, earns it. He who doesn't, pays it."

It is worth taking some time to understand compound interest. More importantly, it is worth taking some time to make sure that you are actually earning compound interest. All types of interest aren't created equally. Understanding the fundamental difference between them will give you insight into how they can work for or against you. As I've already mentioned, compound interest is interest earned on principal and interest. Interest becomes powerful the more time it's given to grow uninterrupted. Compound interest is simply a function of time and interest rate. The longer your money compounds, the greater the growth.

Compound interest is what you want to earn and what you want to avoid paying. When you earn compound interest, it works as the illustration above reveals. You're earning more and more as time goes on. But when you are paying compound interest (as with a credit card that you do not pay off the balance on each month), it can quickly eat up your wealth.

The Problem

There is a reason that compounding is the first "c" in the wealth equation. The power of exponential growth from compounding works reliably over time. The principle and the math work at all times and in all situations. Simple math and reason can easily illustrate that the principle of compounding pays off royally. However, most people are not experiencing that type of growth in their financial accounts.

Why is that? If compounding is a well-known principle, and produces astounding results, why is it that most people are not getting those results?

It is because, while people may be trying to compound their funds, they are not getting the kind of compounding that I advocate in the wealth equation – uninterrupted compounding.

Don't Disrespect the Eighth Wonder!

Most people will never have the eighth wonder of the world working for them because compounding is interrupted by one of four main things; investment losses, taxes, fees and use of money. These are the same wealth transfers I defined earlier. You need to think long-term and consider the effects of these wealth transfers over all the stages of your life.

Here is a quick review of wealth transfers:

Losses

The definition of risk is the chance for loss. Whenever you experience a loss on an investment, you lose more than just the amount of the loss. You lose earning potential.

Taxes

The future rate of taxes you pay and the future bracket you will be in may change, but taxes are not going away. Any time you pay more taxes than necessary today or in the future, you interrupt the compounding curve.

Fees

Not only do fees impede growth, but they also work against you even when your account suffers a loss in value.

Use of Money

Any time you use a dollar, you don't just lose that dollar. You also lose what that dollar could have earned you over your lifetime. The fact that most people are taught to save money during the accumulation phase, and then spend it down in retirement, guarantees that they will never get true, uninterrupted compound interest for life.

Expanding the Penny Example

In the penny example, there was nothing working against the exponential growth of compound interest. In people's actual experience, any and all of the four wealth transfers can interrupt the compounding process.

Imagine that three times during the 30 days (on day 5, 15 and 25), your pennies did not double. That loss would have interrupted the compounding process, and your final amount would have fallen from $5,368,709 to $671,089. Interestingly, only $42,025 was lost due to the penny not doubling on those three days. However, the additional $4,697,620 loss was the effect of interrupting the compounding process.

Let's also consider taxes. In this same example, you pay a 15% tax on the growth of your money. This 15% tax would reduce your account balance from $5,368,709 to $559,732. Even though you only paid $182,736 in total taxes, they caused a reduction in the account balance of $4,808,977.

Imagine if that tax was higher than 15%!

Or, let's presume that there was a 2% fee paid to the person who was managing the penny compounding process. That fee would have interrupted the compounding process, and your balance at the end would have decreased from $5,368,709 all the way down to $2,988,313.

It may be hard to believe, but a 2% fee eliminated over two million dollars. Interrupting the compounding process can be very costly.

Lastly, let's imagine that you need to use some of that money. Twice during the 30 days (on the 15th and 25th day), you have an urgent need to pull $100 for some emergency. Again, it is only a relatively small amount of money that you have used, but the effect of interrupting the compounding process is significant. Your account balance would end up with $2,088,709. The use of that $200 costs you $3,280,000!

You can see that individually the effect of each of the four types of wealth transfers can be overwhelming. Unfortunately, they seldom work against you singly. You may experience losses, taxes, fees and emergency needs simultaneously.

Let's run the numbers one more time and include all these wealth transfers. This time, however, we'll allow them to interrupt the compounding process in a cumulative way. In this final example, the pennies won't double on day 5, 15 or 25, which represents "losses." We'll use a tax rate of 15% and include a 2% fee. For this example, you won't take out any money because any *use* could actually cause your final number to be negative! Your ultimate take-home number at the end of the 30 days tallies up to $51,368. This is a fraction of $5,368,709.

NO INTERRUPTIONS	LOSSES	15% TAX	2% FEE	LOSSES & TAXES & FEES
$5,368,709	$671,089	$559,732	$2,988,313	$51,368

Before you confidently decide to take the compounding penny, do the due diligence necessary to account for any interruptions. You would have been far better off taking the million dollars on day one when wealth transfers are considered.

Most people and financial planners alike don't take the time to do these basic calculations that reveal the devastating effects wealth transfers have on their financial plans.

It has been my experience that most people know they are losing some portion of their gains, but they are regularly a bit stunned to see how great that loss actually is over time. They are not only losing that money, but as all of these examples show, they are losing much more due to the compound-interrupting effect.

By now, you are aware of this effect and can turn these compounded losses into compounding gains. Your first priority should be to maximize the efficiency of your money by finding dollars that are being lost to any wealth transfers. There are almost always many more dollars to be found than you originally anticipate. Once you've found a powerful stream of money, you can set that stream up to earn uninterrupted compound interest for the rest of your life.

Instead of chasing a high ROR, it's better to have a long-term mindset, and put your money somewhere it can grow without investment losses, taxes or hidden fees.

It's better to have a strategy in place so you can use your money without interrupting its ability to compound. The goal is simple. Compound your money in an uninterrupted way for the rest of your life. Let's call this lifetime *uninterrupted compounding.*

Many people who follow a typical financial planning model simply will not get lifetime uninterrupted compounding. Typical financial planning begins with creating an account where you add funds for many years. But, you will ultimately spend from this account, too.

These plans guarantee you will not get lifetime uninterrupted compound interest because they assume, at some point, you will take money out. At whatever point you begin to spend, you lose the benefit of compounding on the amount spent and lose the power of lifetime uninterrupted compounding.

It doesn't have to be this way.

It's possible to create an account in which you accumulate and grow money that can provide income without taking any money out of the account. In this way, you can get true, lifetime uninterrupted compounding.

Compared to What?

By far, the response I most often get when I explain to people that they can be assured of getting an uninterrupted, 4% ROR is: "That's not very good." People don't tend to think that a 4% ROR is a very good deal. My question to them, which I learned to ask from Todd Langford, the founder of Truth Concepts, is always this; "It's not very good compared to what?" There must be something you are comparing that number to in order to determine that it's not very good.

When I talk about a 4% actual ROR, people generally make a comment about market-based investments which advertise an 8% average ROR. So let's compare the two; a 4% actual ROR versus the advertised 8% average ROR.

Let's compare a 4% actual ROR to a period from 1998 to 2016 (a 19 year period) when the Standard and Poor's 500 index (S&P) averaged right around 8%. (It's a commonly held assumption that the S&P will return an average of 7-9% over long periods of time.) We'll start with the average number. If you put $1,000 in the S&P, and it "averaged" (as Wall Street advertises) an 8% return, you would expect to have $4,316 at the end of 19 years.

However, since you know that average and actual ROR are different, you need to calculate a more accurate number by calculating the ROR each year, including years in which the return was negative. When you do this, you find that you end up with only $3,278. This is a 6.45% return.

In addition to the above calculation, you need to factor in taxes. Let's use a tax bracket of 15%. By doing this, you further reduce your final number to $2,446 and reduce your ROR to 4.82%. But, we're not quite done. You still need to account for fees. Once you uncover and calculate for a 2% fee, you end up with an actual total of $1,734 and an actual ROR of 2.94%.

COMPOUND, S&P, TAXES AND FEES

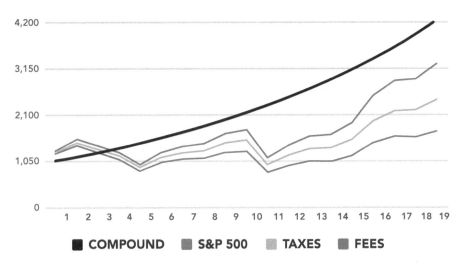

■ COMPOUND   ■ S&P 500   ■ TAXES   ■ FEES

So in summary, in this example, the S&P returned an average of about 8%. That represents an actual year over year return of 6.45%. Taxes reduce that return to 4.82%, and fees further reduce it to 2.94%.

See what happens?

When you compare an advertised 8% average ROR, (which in my example I've demonstrated is really 2.94%), with a 4% actual ROR, you come up with a number that isn't as competitive as it may have appeared. There are many other factors that you have to consider as it relates to lifetime compounding. Many of these benefits are included in an ideal account which I will describe in a later chapter.

Here are eight vital questions to ask yourself about where you put your money.

1. Will your money be safe as it earns lifetime compounding?

2. Do you have a strategy to best use your money without hurting its lifetime growth?

3. Does your money have any guarantees to get lifetime compounding?

4. How are fees being factored into your wealth?

5. Is your lifetime compounding potentially impacted by a government or regulatory change?

6. Is lifetime compounding passive or does it take active management?

7. Will your lifetime compounding continue to grow if something happens to you like a disability or death?

8. How will taxes (present or future) affect your lifetime compounding?

Compounding reveals its power over time. The greater the time period it is allowed to work, the greater effect it will produce. Allow me to explain this with another example.

Flat or Round?

When one of my mentors asked me whether the world was flat or round, I thought it was a pretty foolish question. When he went on to say he could prove that the world is flat, I realized that there was probably some important lesson coming up.

"If we go out on the plains, to a beach or a desert somewhere, I could set up survey equipment and prove that a fairly large stretch of land was perfectly flat," he said. "But, if I took you out to the middle of the ocean and measured a much larger distance of the surface, we would be able to confirm some sort of gentle curve, but certainly nothing like a circle. It is only if you measure immense distances that it becomes clear the world is round."

Compound interest is similar. In the early years that you earn uninterrupted compounding, the growth may seem insignificant enough that it's not even noticeable. However, if you measure it not over years, but over decades, it looks truly stunning.

Earning vs. Paying

You have now learned the powerful concepts of compound interest, but did you know there are other kinds of interest? Knowing and understanding how they work open up many opportunities for you to be more efficient.

Simple Interest

Unlike compound interest, simple interest earns or pays interest on just the principal. In a true, simple-interest calculation, the original principal doesn't increase or decrease. Another way to think of simple interest is "interest only." Interest only is not particularly profitable when earning interest. It doesn't have the exponential power that compound interest does because the interest you earn is only on your original principal.

However, simple interest can be advantageous when paying interest. If you are paying simple interest in order to gain control over principal and you are earning more on the principal than you are paying to control it, you are really starting to gain mastery over your money.

Amortized Interest

Amortized interest is the interest calculated on paying interest and principal during a certain period of time. Amortized interest works in the opposite way compound interest works. Instead of your interest being paid on an increasing principal, your interest is paid on a decreasing principal amount. The payments reduce the amount of principal as well as cover the interest for that period.

When paying interest, it can be to your advantage to use an amortized loan. You pay less in total interest over the life of the loan. In contrast to simple interest, your payment will be higher and you ultimately end up paying off the liability.

Stopping Compounding Interest

Let's look at another example.

Let's see what happens when someone pays $35,000 in cash for a brand new car, keeping opportunity costs in mind. In this example we will assume you can earn 4% interest.

By paying cash, you don't have to pay any interest to a car dealer or bank. Many people stop there and say that was a good purchase because they avoided paying interest. The question that needs to be asked is what was the true cost of paying cash?

If the cash buyer would have left their money to grow at 4% they would have $42,583 after five years. After 10 years, that $35,000 would have grown to over $50k, $110k after 30 years and over $365k after 60 years.

What was the true cost of paying cash? It depends. Over five years paying cash cost $7,583 in interest. Over 60 years the decision to pay cash cost $333,187 in interest. When you pay cash for anything, you're giving up what that dollar could have earned you over your lifetime.

This is only the purchase of one car! Can you imagine the money people are losing unknowingly and unnecessarily on multiple car purchases over their entire life? This is only on a purchase that is paid back over five years! Imagine the amount of money people are losing on longer term purchases?

I understand, for many there is peace-of-mind in not having a car payment or any debt. Do not fool yourself. There is an opportunity cost to paying cash for things. Over long periods of time, that can be a significant amount of money.

Just to be clear, I'm not making this point because I want to encourage people to pay for major purchases by using credit rather than cash. That is not my point at all. I am uncovering and illustrating a money truth that you need to be aware of in order to minimize wealth transfers or losses that come from *using* your money. It's not just what you buy that is important, but how you buy it.

Remember, the idea I keep circling around to in this book is that every dollar lost is compounded by the fact that you are not only losing that dollar but losing what that dollar could have earned you over your lifetime.

One phrase I picked up from Nelson Nash in his book *Becoming Your Own Banker* is the following: "You finance everything you purchase." What he is saying is you will either pay interest by getting a loan or you will lose interest you could've earned by paying cash. For example, by paying cash for my car, I didn't pay any interest. But, assuming I could have earned 4% over 30 years my $10,000 would have been worth over $32,000. In 60 years, my $10,000 would have grown to over $105,000!

Many people are stunned when they see how much ground they can make up by minimizing their current losses. It's equally thrilling to many people when they see how sure and stable their future could be by maximizing their gains. Those two aspects of efficiency (minimizing losses and maximizing gains) are powerful, but I want to turn your attention to the third part of efficiency for a moment. That third part is mastering control of your money.

5

Mastering Unhindered Control

As important and powerful as uninterrupted compounding is, the second "c" in the wealth equation reveals itself to be even more consequential. The second "c" is control. The more I talk with and assist people, the more I realize the importance of control. I see that control is missing from many people's strategies. By the end of this chapter, I sincerely hope that you gain some valuable insight about how powerful it can be to gain and exercise control.

The Explosive Power of Control.

In the last chapter (when I talked about the exponential growth that uninterrupted compounding produces), I was describing an internal ROR. Internal ROR is the return you receive before factoring in taxes, fees or anything else. The exponential shape of a compounding curve is something that will reliably be produced by an investment if you simply reinvest the returns and allow the investment to continue to compound over time without interruption.

Compounding is a Passive Long-term Strategy.

You don't have to do anything for compounding to work for you. In fact, that's kind of the point of compounding. If you don't do anything to interrupt the inherent, reliable and productive process, it will do the work for you.

Control works in just the opposite way. Control is about doing things. Control is about doing everything you can to affect the external ROR. This is the rate you actually end up with after taxes, fees, inflation and opportunities are taken into consideration. Because control is an active not a passive investment strategy, there is no real way to chart its effectiveness. It doesn't follow an incremental or exponential curve.

The better you become, the more mastery you gain, and the greater return you can produce. That can happen in large leaps and bounds. The potential growth of your investment is not just exponential but explosive. For example, a person might invest in a property, make improvements to it, exercise control to increase its value and then sell it for a multiple of what they invested into it. Flipping a house is admittedly an active investment strategy; it takes some thought and work. But, if you know what you are doing (you've gained mastery over the elements you can control), it can be very profitable in a relatively short amount of time.

If you look at your money through the lens of control, you won't just see your money as savings. You will see it as capital. It is not just savings sitting there growing, waiting to be used sometime in the future. It's capital that represents your greatest opportunity for reaching your highest potential and accomplishing your **Why**.

Remember what I said earlier about your greatest financial need?

Your greatest financial need is to *use* your money. You will use far more money than you save, so learning how to use money will have a greater effect than saving more money. Use of money or access to capital is your greatest financial strategy. Yet, few people out there are teaching their clients about the very best and most efficient way to control and use their capital.

When was the last time someone showed you an effective strategy to use your money?

Compounding may be, as Einstein is credited with saying, the eighth wonder of the world. But, as a principle of building wealth, the control of capital blows compounding out of the water! Which is why I consider "unhindered control" to be the ninth wonder of the world!

Investing at "The Center"

Control enables you to remove key risks and take any intentional action necessary to multiply your money. Your control over an investment diminishes the further you get from the center. You always want to be as close to the center of an investment as possible. The more control you have, the more potential you have to actively minimize losses and maximize gains. Let's use Facebook as an example.

Mark Zuckerberg, the co-founder and CEO of Facebook, is at the center of Facebook as an investment.

He created it and exercises the greatest control over it. It was, in essence, his idea, his sweat equity and his investment of time and money. He has the freedom and the responsibility to identify where losses are happening and take steps to stem those losses. He can define where potential gains exist and move the company to realize those gains. He exercises control that minimizes losses and maximizes gains. He has the greatest, most unhindered control over the investment and makes the most money from its success.

One step away from the center there are relatively few direct investors.

Early on, they contributed the capital necessary to develop and grow Facebook. As initial investors, these individuals have some control over the direction of the company. But, their ability to influence is certainly less than Zuckerberg's, and their profit, while very significant, is less than his as well.

If you take another step away from the center, there are shareholders or people who own Facebook stock.

Since Facebook went public, a large number of people have purchased stock in the company. While it is true that Facebook has a responsibility to produce returns for its shareholders, this group of people has very little control over the workings of Facebook.

They can do very little to affect the return on their investment. They are simply betting that those closer to the center will do their job well. Their portion of the profits is significantly less than the initial investors and far less than Zuckerberg's.

Taking yet another step away from the center, there are people who invest in mutual funds.

These mutual funds hold Facebook stock. Mutual fund owners have the least influence over the profitability of Facebook. They have very little control over increasing the return of their investment. The fund manager ultimately decides whether to hold onto the stock or liquidate it. People who invest in mutual funds have the least control, and by far, have the smallest ROR from their investment. Can you see the progression?

Every step you take away from the center gives up a measure of control to the people closer to the center. With diminished control come diminished returns.

Can you see the problem?

Most people are investing in mutual funds, where they have the least control and make the smallest portion of the profits. When you acknowledge the explosive power of control, you can learn to exercise it. When you begin to exercise it, you will find yourself pulling away from doing what everyone else is doing on the less profitable edges and leaning in toward the more profitable center. When you master control over your capital, you don't have to go looking for profitable investment opportunities. When you control your capital, opportunities will be more available to you.

Mastering Control Over "The Big Nine"

There are nine elements over which you need to gain control. These elements are the things you can do to maximize the efficiency of your financial plan. All of them affect your external (or actual) ROR and all of them are worth your attention.

1. Keep Your Money Safe.

"You have to take greater risks to get greater returns" is an assumption that has cost people dearly over the years. It's not true, and it's not necessary.

The people who are mastering control of their money will rid themselves of this assumption. Replace that assumption with this one: There are ample opportunities out there to get a good ROR which come with little to no risk. It's your role to uncover and take advantage of them.

One of the things that tends to be true about us as humans is that we generally find what we look for. For example, if you tune yourself to look for risky investments that are likely to make and lose lots of money for you, that's what you'll find. But, if you tune yourself to look for solid investments that will generate exponential returns and lose none of your gains, that is exactly what you will find. The other assumption you need to let go of is the ingrained and long taught belief that average ROR represents a real number which you can use to determine the value of an investment.

As I've demonstrated to you earlier, the average ROR overstates gains and understates losses to such a degree that it actually tells you very little about the actual ROR. Assume instead that the average ROR is a sales tactic. Take control of the information you obtain when you make financial decisions. Do your due diligence in order to find out, as closely as possible, the actual ROR. Take into account fees, losses, taxes and anything else not represented by the phantom, average ROR percentage.

You may need the assistance of someone who has access to the calculators and the inside information you need to uncover fees and other wealth transfers, but it is well worth your time to seek out that person. If average ROR is the only compelling reason to put your money into an investment, you are likely better off to pass on it. It's difficult to put a dollar amount on it, but it is worthwhile to ask this question: "What is the value of safety?"

If I have the choice between having my money in a place that is safe versus a place that is exposed to potential loss, what is the added value of that safe place?

2. Keep Your Money Liquid.

Liquidity means having your money available to deploy when you do come across a safe and profitable investment. This will begin to happen more frequently as you master control. Liquidity is about having your money available, not "tied up" where you can't get to it when an opportunity arises.

The explosive profit potential that comes from investing your capital is very often a function of timing. Real estate was available at significantly undervalued prices post 2008. That historic opportunity was completely missed by millions of people whose investment money was tied up in 401(k)s and other restricted accounts. Most people would agree that they need to have an emergency fund so that money is available to cover unforeseen expenses. However, few people think about having a capital fund so their money is available to fund unanticipated opportunities.

Often, financial institutions will attempt to incentivize you to invest your money with them by offering a slightly higher ROR if you agree to leave your money with them for longer terms. You'll get a better rate on a 10-year CD than on a 12-month CD. Remember that if you give up liquidity by tying up your money for a certain period of time, you'll give up control and will be forced to let opportunities pass by. What is the value of keeping your money liquid? It is better to keep as much of your money liquid as possible unless (and until) there are productive, safe alternatives available to you.

3. Keep Your Money Leverageable.

Leverage is one of the most important tools you can gain mastery over in order to build wealth. The effective use of leverage is all about control. A healthy fear of leverage is a very good thing because a person can certainly get over-leveraged and cause themselves financial harm. However, an irrational fear of leverage (either avoiding it at all costs or somehow thinking that you aren't smart enough or can't become savvy enough to make it work for you), is just as damaging. To effectively take advantage of leverage, you need to have a secure grasp on two ideas – "collateral" and "control costs."

Collateral refers to anything that you may put up as security for a loan. Let's say that you borrow $10,000 and put up your car as collateral. Technically, the car remains yours. You drive it and use it just as you always have. You do not lose the use of the car in any way. It is only if you do not pay the loan back (according to the terms) that the car becomes the property of the person or financial institution you borrowed the money from.

I'll show you the intricacies of collateralization in upcoming chapters. Collateral belongs in this discussion of control because it is a way to have your money working for you in more than one place at a time. If you have significant capital in a place where you can use it as collateral, that capital can be growing for you there at the same time. It can also be leveraged to produce gains for you in another place. In this situation, you are not taking your money out of that place; you are simply borrowing against your own money. This is a level of control that you wouldn't want to enter into lightly or without confidence. But, it is well worth the time to learn how to control your money in this highly profitable way.

Control Cost is the term I use to describe the amount of money you spend in order to control and/or gain a larger amount of money. One of the most profitable industries in the world is banking. For example, a bank pays you 1% on a $1,000 deposit. Then they charge someone else 4% to borrow that same money. The 1% they pay you is their control cost. It's the amount they had to pay in order to control your $1,000. It costs them $10 to control $1,000. Would you pay 1% in order to earn 4%? Bankers answer "yes" to that question all day long.

All of the benefits of leverage and collateralization are nullified if your investment funds are in vehicles where they cannot be leveraged. It is in your best interest to keep your money available to work for you by housing it in a place where it can function as collateral. Think long and hard about this question. What's the value of being able to leverage your money? All things being equal, what value is added if you can use leverage to gain higher returns, control larger assets or reduce your liabilities?

4. Keep Your Money Private.

Unfortunately, we live in a lawsuit-happy world in which there are many people who want to get their hands on your money. For any number of reasons, you may find yourself in a situation where someone may make an attempt to get a judgment against you and take your wealth. Keeping this in mind as you master your financial plan is key. Some of your money is easily available to creditors. It is low-hanging fruit. The garnishing of wages is one of the most simple, straightforward things they can do to get their hands on your money.

But, there are places you can save and grow your money which are much better protected than others. You owe it to yourself to take a good, hard look at where you put your funds and choose places where your money is safe from potential creditors. What is it worth to you to know that your money is really yours, private and not easy for other people to access?

5. Protect Your Money from Taxes.

Gaining control over the money you lose to taxes is so important that I devote an entire chapter to this issue. At this point, I just want to say that there are entities that intend to get at a portion of your wealth. Their assumption is that a portion of your money belongs to them (or for them to use for the common good).

You literally cannot afford to try to build significant wealth without an aggressive and effective tax strategy. It ought to be your goal to have as much of your money growing tax-free and being distributed to you as tax-free as possible.

It is not enough to defer taxes, postponing both the calculation and the payment of the tax to a later date. It is important to get free of them to the legal extent possible. You can have significant control over the amount of taxes you pay. You can manage your tax liability in the present in such a way that you get free of it in the future. Qualified plans with a match can be a good place for someone to put some of their money for retirement. It's good to know how these matches work, how they affect your money and how they perform over the short and long-term.

But, individuals that invest above the company match could incur some very costly wealth transfers depending on what the future holds. Protecting your money from the eroding influence of taxation is, by its very nature, an ongoing process. There is a high-stakes game going on and the rules are always being tweaked. You'll need to get savvy in order to win. Your best bet is to accumulate your money in places where it can grow and be accessible without any exposure to taxation at all. What is the value of having your money growing tax-free and coming to you tax-free?

6. Protect Your Money from Fees.

Administrative expenses, advisory fees and load fees (front-end and back-end) are some of the more easily identifiable fees you may encounter as you evaluate various financial vehicles. However, many fees can be difficult to uncover. Technically, they are probably enumerated somewhere in the fine print, but they are seldom articulated clearly or prominently disclosed.

If you look for them carefully, you'll find fees everywhere. A financial advisor might charge a fee each year that is based on a percentage of the money being managed. Mutual funds may charge a fee at the time of initial investment or when the investment is sold. One method to generate revenue is to charge marketing fees which get wrapped up into the expense ratio so they don't appear as management fees.

Retirement accounts often have built-in management fees. All of this means that you are most likely paying appreciably more in fees than you think you are. Assuming you've picked up a recurring theme in this book, you know that the effect of even small fees may cost you dearly.

There are two kinds of fees. Fixed-fees and percentage-based fees.

Fixed-fees are not based on an account balance. With a fixed-fee, you pay a certain amount regardless of how much money you have invested. Whether you have $100,000 or $1 million in an account, the fee is the same.

Percentage-based fees are the opposite. With percentage-based fees, your fees are a percentage of the amount of money someone is managing for you. At a rate of 1%, your fee would be $1,000 on a $100,000 investment. Assuming the same rate of 1%, the fee would jump to $10,000 on a $1 million investment.

It may be uncomfortable or awkward to ask questions in order to get an accurate understanding of what fees exist and how they can affect your actual return. But, it's your money that we are talking about here. It's your life and your **Why** that are at stake. You can't exercise control over what you don't know exists. It is in your best interest to assume that there may be additional fees hidden in the investments you are considering than are readily apparent. Do the work necessary to avoid as many fees as possible.

7. Protect Your Money from Inflation.

Inflation produces an overall increase in the price of goods and services year by year. The product that cost you $10 last year, may cost $10.30 this year and $10.60 the following year. Inflation erodes the purchasing power of your money. It is important that your wealth grows at a rate that keeps up with or exceeds inflation. If it does not, then you are actually losing the wealth building battle.

It's worth noting that what I've just described is the effect of inflation, not inflation itself. Technically, inflation is an increase in the money supply. When the Federal Reserve prints money, it increases the number of dollars that are in the financial system. All of those newly created dollars borrow some of their value from the existing dollars that are already in the system. The effect of all of those new dollars is to decrease the value of your existing dollars. Inflation functions as a silent, or stealth tax.

At the end of the day, there is little you (or I) can do to stop those who are in control of our monetary system from using their inflationary power. What you can do (and should do) is factor the effects of inflation into your financial planning. It is important to ensure that the actual ROR is positive even after factoring in inflation.

It is also important to keep an eye on inflation because it can get out of control. Historically, there have been some pretty devastating periods during which inflation rates soared. In that type of an environment, the people who had control over their money could turn their dollars into real property (precious metals, real estate, fine art, etc.) which also inflated in value. Those who did not have control simply had to stand by as inflation eroded the purchasing power of their wealth.

Whether it involves negotiating the known effects of low level inflation or being prepared for the unknown turbulent possibilities of runaway inflation, protecting your money from inflation is a responsibility you should take seriously.

8. Protect Your Money from Restrictions and Compulsions.

There are a number of financial vehicles which put restrictions on the amount of money you can put into them. These vehicles often have compulsions such as deadlines by which you must take your money (distributions) out of them. You don't have control over putting as much as you want into them, and you don't have control over leaving your money there to grow as long as you want. Restrictions and compulsions are indications that these vehicles don't have your best interests at heart. Whenever there are restrictions involved, those restrictions tend to limit your potential ROR. Whenever there are compulsions, those too, will tend to work against you.

If you recognize that you are in control and exercise that control effectively, you'll be looking for places where you can deploy as much of your capital as you see fit. Money can work profitably for you as long as you choose to let it do so. Remember, you want to play "the game" your way. There are many financial vehicles available that don't place limitations and demands on your money. You are free to politely pass on situations that corral your money and cause you to give up control. With the knowledge you have gained, you can set your money free.

9. Protect Your "Human Life Value."

I am going to finish this list of "The Big Nine" with what I believe to be the most important element. "Human life value" is a term used to describe your maximum, financial potential. I've said it before; "you are your greatest asset," and I consider it my true life's mission to help as many people as possible see and reach their highest potential.

With your highest potential in mind, not only do you need to put your wealth in a place that you control today, you also need to insure that an unexpected or even tragic incident doesn't eliminate that potential in the future. The reality for most people is that their ability to earn an income today and in the future is their greatest financial asset. Many people do not insure that ability, and the ones that do may be doing so inefficiently. They may be incurring some unnecessary wealth transfers in the way they protect themselves.

There are four things that may affect human life value. They are health problems, disability, long-term care and death. In most cases, insurance is the most efficient way to protect and cover your human life value in each of these areas. Think of insurance companies as professionals that manage risk. However, just because insurance is the most efficient way to protect your human life value, it doesn't mean all insurance is good. There are striking differences between companies and between insurance products. You need to do your best to maximize your efficiency by properly managing your risk. Be careful not to over insure or overpay for insurance. Doing so, amounts to wasting money that could be utilized elsewhere.

While only one of the four things that affect human life value is certain (death), making sure you efficiently protect and plan for all of the four is vital. From a purely monetary standpoint, it will cost you much less to insure yourself against these possibilities ahead of time than it will to navigate them if or when they occur. Remember, you are your greatest financial asset! You want to ensure that your future goals and your *Why* happen. You also want to put every single one of your dollars in a place that helps optimize your human life value today and maximize its potential in the future.

The ROI of a Golf Club

I want to end this chapter with a not-so-simple question. What's the real value of control? How can you put a numeric value on the elements of control? Return-on-investment (or ROI) is a term those in the financial industry use to reflect the value of something. What is the true ROI of taking risk off the table and having your money available for key opportunities? The answer is that it fundamentally depends on your mastery. It depends on how well you control it.

If you're a very average golfer like me, the ROI of a golf club is zero. Actually, it's less than that because every time I play golf, I pay money to do so. The return on my investment is a negative. However, if you're Phil Mickelson, the return on that same golf club could be over a million dollars!

Even though I am not a great golfer, I could take the game of golf and make it ROI positive by how I intentionally use my time. For instance, I could spend time with a potential client, and while golfing, develop a close business relationship which would easily pay for the time and cost of golfing. The ROI a golf club produces is dependent on how good of a golfer you are or how you use your time while on the course.

It's the same with money. Control might be the ninth wonder of the world, but it's nothing special if you don't learn how to master it and use it for your benefit. If I am going to help you see and reach your highest potential, it's imperative that I show you how to exercise control over more and more of your wealth.

6

Taxes

Let me give you an example of a hypothetical financial situation. The situation I'm thinking of involves a person who earns $35,000 per year but spends $40,000. As a result of the income/expense gap they have been incurring for some time, they have over $200,000 in credit card debt. You would probably agree with me that they are in poor financial shape. In order to get to a better place, they would either need to dramatically increase their income or dramatically reduce their spending in order to aggressively knock down that debt.

Let me ask you a question. Would you take investment advice from this person or hire them as your financial advisor? Would it make sense to have this person give you counsel on how you should structure your money so that it works most effectively for you?

I can almost hear you screaming, "NO WAY!"

Let me ask you another question. How would you respond if this person invited you to go into business with them? Would you enter into a partnership with them in which you put up all the money, took all the risk and paid all the fees while they retained the right to change their ownership-stake in the business and change the rules at any time? Not likely.

No one in their right mind would ever consider this! Yet, millions of people are putting their hard-earned money in this type of partnership every single year.

If you add eight zeros to the numbers I gave you, this example turns into a snapshot of the U.S. Government's financial situation. At the time this book was written, the U.S. was earning almost $3.5 trillion, spending about $4 trillion and is roughly $20 trillion in debt. At usdebtclock.org you can see what these numbers are currently. These numbers are only getting worse as our national debt increases, and they don't include national, unfunded liabilities.

I wholeheartedly believe that government taxation and regulation is the primary risk to your wealth.

Instead of protecting your money from this risk, you are effectively earmarking a portion of your money to hand over to the government any time you are using tax-deferred plans. Tax-deferred plans are also called "qualified plans" because they are in a category of employer-sponsored retirement plans that qualify for special tax treatment by the IRS (Internal Revenue Service).

I actually prefer to call them "postponement plans" because, rather than dealing with the effects of taxation, they encourage people to kick the can down the road and postpone both the calculation and payment of taxes. The most common of these plans are traditional 401(k)s, 403(b)s, traditional or simple IRAs (Individual Retirement Accounts) and SEPs (Simple Employee Pension Accounts). These plans became popular in the 1980s as many companies moved away from defined (traditional) pension plans. Many people invest most, if not all, of their financial future in these types of plans without really understanding the consequences of them.

These plans are represented as being "tax-sheltered." They offer people the opportunity to put pre-tax dollars into them and have those dollars grow without being taxed. The effect is that people get to deduct their contributions (which lessens their tax burden in that year) and defer taxes on the growth (which further lessens their immediate tax burden). This makes them very attractive on the front-end.

But remember, you want to be as efficient as possible throughout the whole process (growth, income and legacy). As with many things in life, the front-end may look good. The back-end, however, can be particularly unattractive.

There are two important things people are unaware of or ignore when they put money into these plans. First, their money is not very liquid. It is locked away and, in most cases, can't be accessed without a penalty. Second, they will have to pay taxes on both the original contribution and the growth at some time in the future. The opportunity cost of relinquishing your money into these financial vehicles is enormous.

I want to cover several compelling reasons for you to take tax-deferred plans off of your investment options list. What follows are three ways in which these plans actually hinder you in your attempt to reach your financial goals.

1. The Unknown

Earlier in the book, I mentioned that there are two things that go into the amount of taxes you pay. One is the rate you pay and the other is the threshold (or bracket) you are in when you pay them. It can be tempting to believe that you don't have very much control over the rate you pay or the bracket you are in. The government sets those numbers, so they are out of your control, right?

Not necessarily. Working with good data you can create an effective tax plan. You can influence both the tax rate you pay and your bracket. This is how businesses routinely make a lot of money but pay a minimal amount in taxes.

Profitable businesses employ tax code experts that know very clearly where the lines are drawn, where the thresholds lie and what the rules are that go into the algorithm-like calculations that generate the dollar amount they need to pay in taxes. Because they know what the rules are and how the playing field is set up, they can work the numbers in their favor to reduce the business' tax burden (both legally and ethically).

But what does a business fear? In what environment do businesses least like to be? When do the markets and investors get jittery about their ability to survive and make a profit?

It is when there are unknowns. If a business doesn't know what its tax or regulatory burdens are, it cannot exercise control over its business. It cannot set itself up to take advantage of (or mitigate against the damage of) taxes and regulations.

Any successful and profitable business, if offered the choice between a known tax rate/tax bracket in the present, or an unknown rate/tax bracket in the future, would choose the known over the unknown. It's all about control. Your ability to do what is necessary in order to minimize losses and maximize gains is contingent on the information and knowledge you have to work with.

Essentially, when someone puts money into a tax-deferred plan, they lose nearly all control. They lose it for a really long time. Ultimately, they will have to pay tax on whatever they withdraw, at whatever the tax rate is, based on whatever tax bracket they find themselves in. To make matters worse, even if they don't want to, they are forced to take their required minimum distributions (RMD) and pay taxes on them when they reach a certain age.

When you choose a tax-deferred plan, you surrender a significant amount of control which will affect your ability to maximize your earning potential.

2. The Harvest

My home state of Wisconsin may be known for its dairy industry, but it also produces a whole lot of corn to feed those cattle. Imagine that a corn farmer has to plant one truckload of seed corn in order to harvest ten truckloads of corn for market. Imagine also, that the farmer has the opportunity to choose between two different ways he could pay taxes on his corn production.

The first option is to pay a known tax on the one truckload of seed corn today. The second option is to pay an unknown tax on the ten truckloads of market corn he harvests at the end of the year. Which option do you think he would choose?

I'd propose that he should choose the tax on the single truckload of seed corn today. By doing so, he would be dealing with a known tax rate. And, if he does some good tax-planning, he may be able to reduce the impact of that tax just like the business owner we discussed earlier. More importantly, he would be paying the tax on a smaller amount of corn.

When someone chooses a tax-deferred vehicle (over a tax-free vehicle), they choose to pay taxes on the entire harvest in the future rather than on just the seed. That in itself, is reason enough to choose a tax-free vehicle over a tax-deferred one.

They are also choosing to bet that the rate they will pay in the future and the tax bracket they will be in will be lower than it is today. Let's take a look at the odds involved in that bet.

3. The Gamble

When you are faced with the choice of paying taxes now or postponing them to the future, you are essentially making a bet. You would be emboldened to take that bet if you had reason to believe one of a few things. That you would be in a lower tax-bracket in the future. That the tax rate would be lower in the future, or both. I think the assumption that you will be taxed less in the future is incorrect. Making this assumption is essentially predicting that you will be poorer in the future. You owe it to yourself to talk to some of the current generation of retirees who were sold on the idea that they would retire in a lower tax bracket and invested in tax-deferred funds. What you will find is that a number of things conspired to cause them to regret that decision.

For one thing, income from these plans is disbursed as "earned income" which is taxed at a higher rate than capital gains, dividends or interest income. Additionally, a number of exemptions and credits (child credits, retirement savings credits, etc.) probably ended when they retired. Those credits reduced their taxable income while they were working. Finally, when retirees reach a certain age they are impacted by required minimum distributions from their tax-deferred accounts. These RMDs may increase over time, and you are nearly guaranteed to be in at least as high a tax bracket as you are today. Take the time to work the numbers and consider all the factors involved. You may not come to the same exact conclusion I do, but at least you'll know what the potential impact may be.

To see an example of how the tax rate and threshold can be changed in order to cover what the government needs to fund, consider this. In 1941, the top individual tax rate was 81% and the highest threshold was $5 million.

A person in 1941 who made $200,000 could be reasonably confident that they didn't need to worry about being in a higher tax bracket or paying a higher rate. Unfortunately for them, one year later, the government raised the top tax rate to 88%, and the threshold was lowered down to $200,000. Not only did the top wage earners have to pay more in taxes, but the threshold was lowered, so considerably more people were added to that bracket. Why did the government make those drastic changes in the tax code? The answer can be boiled down to one word – math.

Leading up to 1942, war had been spreading throughout Europe, Asia and other parts of the world. The mantra for the U.S. Government was "preparedness." Beginning in 1939, a number of preparedness agencies were created to mobilize resources. This included: supplies, food, military hardware and most importantly, money that would be needed to finance the war effort. Military planners calculated how much money would be required to win the war. The calculations revealed an astronomical number. Having done everything that could be done to retool the economy to support the war effort, there was simply no way to pay for the war with the funds at hand. The only way to fund the war effort was to exercise the power of taxation. Americans who earned as little as $500 per year paid income tax at a 23% rate, while those who earned more than $1 million per year paid an all-time high 94% rate!

I'm not promoting any sort of conspiracy theories, making any moral judgments or railing against a greedy government who wanted to plunder and pillage your wealth. I'm just following the math involved. This led me to conclude that, in the long run, taxes will be going up.

Based on the current financial position of the U.S. Government (which I described earlier), the math indicates that three things need to happen:

1. Debt needs to be paid down quickly;

2. Expenses need to decrease significantly (Spending); and

3. Income needs to increase significantly (Taxes).

Let's examine these three things in greater detail.

1. Can debt be paid off?

When this book was being written, the national debt was approximately 20 trillion dollars and increasing by over two billion dollars per day. These numbers can be so far beyond our ability to comprehend that they lose any real meaning. The math, however, puts it in a pretty clear perspective. It is mathematically impossible for the government to pay off its current debt.

2. Can expenses be decreased?

In 2016, roughly 76% of every tax dollar was needed to pay for Social Security, Medicare, Medicaid, and interest on the national debt. The Government Accountability Office estimates that, by 2020, it could take 92% of every tax dollar to fund those same line items. These are expenses that we are already committed to. That means a meager eight cents of each tax dollar will go to every other government program.

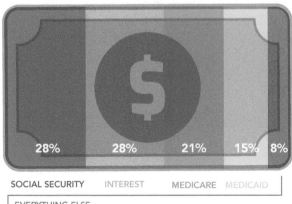

28% SOCIAL SECURITY 28% INTEREST 21% MEDICARE 15% MEDICAID 8% EVERYTHING ELSE

3. Can income be increased?

The majority of collected tax dollars are already spent. They are not available to pay for any of the myriad of other expenses involved in running the government. Simple math indicates that expenses are increasing and will most likely continue to do so in the future. The only way to significantly increase the government's income is to raise taxes.

Does the current financial situation of the U.S. Government, and its projected future needs, indicate that taxes are more likely to go up or down? If they go up, when will it happen and what will be the justification?

Nobody knows. The numeric odds would lead a betting person to pay taxes today and keep as much of that money in a tax-free vehicle as possible. It is vital that your money grows efficiently with the possibility of a changing tax-environment.

If you make a quick evaluation of tax-deferred or qualified plans, using the nine elements of control I enumerated earlier, you find that they don't hold up very well. People ultimately act in a way that is consistent with what they believe. If you believe that future taxes are likely to have a negative impact on your wealth, you should limit or eliminate the money you feed into tax-deferred plans.

7

Controlling Your Money Like a Banker

Banks are the masters of control. The business of banking is essentially taking other people's money (sometimes called OPM) and controlling it for profit. Banks have figured out that they don't have to own capital; they just have to be able to control it. Banking is one of the most profitable industries in the world because they have the best processes for controlling capital. If I've learned anything on my journey, it has been this:

Find those who are having the most success and learn how to do what they are doing.

Instead of resenting how banks are profiting off of your money, you should study them and learn their secrets. This way, you can better control your own capital and even benefit from knowing how to use OPM.

If you can begin to think and act like a banker, you will find yourself experiencing the same type of success that the banking industry does. Thinking like a banker means taking a different view than the one you are used to having. It involves a shift in mindset. Banks think about and use money in a way that is completely opposite from most people. For example, depositing money in a bank is considered an asset by most people. Banks see it as a liability because that money is owed back to the customer. On the flip side, many people see loans as a liability, but the bank sees loans as an asset because money is owed to them by their customers.

1. Flow

Banks direct the flow of money better than other businesses by offering direct deposits. Your money flows through them first before it gets to you. Because of direct deposits, your money sits in the bank and is available for their use until you need access to it.

Wall Street financial institutions figured this out as well, and that's why they did everything they could to facilitate the introduction of 401(k) plans. Money now automatically flows to them from your employer before you ever touch it. The U.S. Government also figured this out many years ago. This is why employers are required to withhold a portion of your gross income to pay taxes, before you see a penny of it. Banks, Wall Street financial institutions and the U.S. Government are all trying their best to get as much of your money flowing to them before it goes to you. They don't need to own it outright, they just need to be able to control it before you do!

You need a process where you can maximize the flow of your money towards you, not away from you.

2. Leverage

The root of leverage is the word "lever." With the use of a lever, you can accomplish vastly more than you can without it. Financial leverage is the act of using OPM to gain a higher return or to control a larger investment than would be possible with your own money. Banks leverage the money deposited to them by turning around and lending it out to others. Let's say you deposit $100 and the bank pays you 1% for the use of that money. The bank's liability is that $100, plus the interest they owe you, which is an additional $1, so their liability is $101.

For the bank to be profitable, they need to loan your money out at a higher interest rate than they are charging you. So let's say they can earn 4%. They take your $100 and loan it to someone else and get back $104. After they pay off their liability to you of $101, they end up with a profit of $3. This $3 may not seem like much of a profit. Remember, bankers have perfected the art of getting your money to flow through them first before it gets to you.

The bank spent $1 to earn $4. While a $3 profit may not seem like much, it's actually a 300% ROI!

	INVESTMENT	PROFIT	ROI
CASH INVESTOR	$100	$4	4%
BANK	$1	$3	300%

They don't have to make a huge profit. They just have to make a little profit on the huge amounts of money that flow through them.

Leverage is powerful. It is indiscriminately powerful and can work as aggressively against someone as it does for them. Goldman Sachs, Lehman Brothers and Bear Stearns were some of the well-established investment banks that became over-leveraged in 2008 and were either bailed out by the U.S. Government or went bankrupt. To guard against that possibility, a bank must always be balancing their judicious use of leverage while maintaining adequate liquidity, proper collateral and making wise investments.

It can be difficult to understand how to use the power of leverage in your financial plan. However, it is vital to consider the big part leverage could play in your personal wealth strategy.

3. Liquidity

Liquidity is the ability to access money. At any given point, a bank needs to have access to enough funds to cover its liabilities, relinquish money to customers and take advantage of any opportunities that arise. Liquidity is important because a bank cannot know precisely what the future holds. There are opportunities and setbacks which regularly occur.

This is one of the differences between the way a banker thinks and the way most other people think. The average person, if they think about liquidity at all, is thinking about setbacks. They want to have enough money available to cover any unexpected expenses. On the other hand, a banker is also looking to have enough money available to take advantage of opportunities.

When you have liquidity, you are able to access money to deal with any setbacks or emergencies without taking on debt which eats away at your wealth. When you have liquidity, or access to money, you also have a reserve in order to take advantage of opportunities that may have a very high value to you.

Having liquidity not only for emergencies, but more importantly, for opportunities, is a function of banking that you as an individual should also adopt.

4. Collateral

Collateral is any asset that a borrower offers as security for a loan. If the borrower does not pay the bank back, the bank takes the asset. Normally, the loan is collateralized with whatever the loan is being used for. A house serves as collateral for a mortgage, a car serves as collateral for a car loan, etc. From a banker's perspective, collateral is all about safety.

Having worked at a bank for four and a half years, I can assure you that banks have no intention of losing money. Requiring collateral for loans is one way to ensure that they don't. Collateral gives the borrower a compelling reason to repay the loan and, if that is not successful, the asset can be sold to cover the remaining balance. Since collateral offers a measure of safety to the lender, collateralized loans typically have significantly lower interest rates than uncollateralized ones. This means banks make considerably less from a loan than a credit card company does. Banks are okay with this because they haven't bought into the greater risk equals greater reward hype.

A banker knows that there is great value in a competitive, but safe, return on their money. They don't want to chase a greater ROR by taking on more risk, and neither should you!

5. Velocity

Velocity describes how the other four concepts (flow, leverage, liquidity and collateral) all work together. The velocity of money is the rate at which money is exchanged from one transaction to another. A high velocity means that your money is turning over often. It means your money is working harder and producing more.

When your paycheck is direct-deposited into your bank, the bank doesn't just let it sit there. It puts the money to work. They loan it out. This allows your money to be doing more work for them. In effect, it is in more than one place at a time. When a bank receives payments on the loans they make, they can also turn around and lend that money back out. It's an efficient process creating more velocity, and ultimately, earning an ever greater return for the bank. The initial deposit can earn multiple times its original value.

A banker's goal is to take every dollar that comes through their door and squeeze as many benefits out of that dollar as possible. While you can't use OPM to the extent that banks do, you can use it more effectively than you may think. You can also adopt some of their best practices and create your own system for controlling money.

Section 3

The Controlled Compounding Strategy™

8

Controlled Compounding

Previously, I explained both of the "c"s in the wealth equation: compounding and control. If I did my job correctly, you now have some appreciation for both of them and the role they can play in helping you craft an efficient and profitable financial plan.

The first "c," uninterrupted compounding, involves harnessing the exponential power of a passive investment strategy to maximize internal ROR. The second "c," unhindered control, involves gaining mastery over the explosive power of an active investment strategy to maximize external ROR. I will now bring these concepts together and show you how to take full advantage of them.

The Big Dilemma

As I moved along in my financial education journey, I became convinced of some bedrock realities. I knew some of the intricacies of how money worked. I knew that I was my greatest asset. And, I knew that my greatest financial need was to use my money. It was obvious that if I was going to reach my highest potential, it was going to require money for education, business, travel and investing.

I also understood the principle of compounding. I knew that if I saved my money instead of using it, my money would grow exponentially. Every dollar that I would spend, even on good things, would interrupt the compounding process.

Have you ever been in a situation where it appears you're stuck between a rock and a hard place? I felt that way, but it was even more frustrating because I knew it wasn't a rock and a hard place. I was stuck between two amazing opportunities that appeared to be mutually exclusive. I couldn't pursue one without pulling the rug out from under the other. And, I wasn't on this journey alone. I had set out to find a better way for my clients. And, here I was with two paths I had growing confidence in, but they seemed to be incompatible.

It's hard to describe what I experienced when it clicked for me. It was like the light came on or the pieces fell into place. I thought, "We can have both! Control and compounding are not mutually exclusive! They can be used in tandem to produce greater results than either was ever capable of separately!"

I call this concept the "Controlled Compounding Strategy™."

Before I give you an overview of controlled compounding, let's go over how people use their money. People can be divided into three groups based on how they pay for things: debtors, savers and maximizers.

1. Debtors

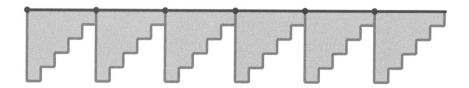

They use up their money to fund their lifestyle. They do not save money, and as a result, if there is an emergency, a necessary major purchase or an investment opportunity, they feel they can't pass up, they borrow. Then, they pay interest and principal until the debt is paid off. When the next financial need presents itself, they repeat the cycle. Debtors take out loans and then pay them back in steps, over time, until they are back to where they were before they took out the loan.

2. Savers

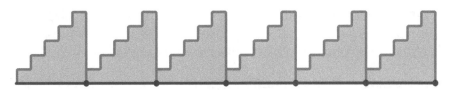

They save up their money so that they do not have to pay interest. If there is a financial need, they simply spend to cover the expense from their savings. Then, they save more in steps over time to replenish their savings. If the situation reoccurs, they repeat the cycle.

Savers avoid paying interest, but they also lose out on earning interest during the period in which they have drained their account and are paying themselves back. However, there is a third way to approach your financial needs.

3. Maximizers

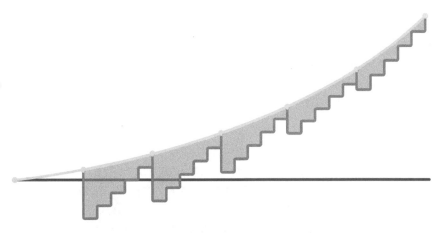

Just like the saver, a maximizer saves in steps. But, if money needs to be spent, they borrow the funds they need using their saved money as collateral. Remember the example of using a car for collateral on a loan? The car continues to be yours. You don't lose the use of the car at all. The same thing is true when you use money for collateral on a loan. Your money never leaves your account; it's unaffected. You continue to earn uninterrupted compound interest while you pay the loan back with amortized interest.

A maximizer uses their money in the most efficient way possible. They leverage their savings through collateralization. In this way, they get the best of both worlds. They get control over the funds they need for emergencies, major purchases or investments while getting uninterrupted compounding on their savings at the same time.

Now that we covered the difference of the three types of people, let's look at exactly how maximizers use controlled compounding as the best long-term savings strategy while using their money today. I will take you through a review of the concepts involved in controlled compounding.

You finance everything you purchase. You either pay interest by purchasing with a loan/credit, or you lose interest you could have earned by paying with cash. Either way, there is a cost to any purchase or investment.

Compound interest grows over time. Amortized interest shrinks over time. Because of this, it can be advantageous to pay amortized interest in order to earn compound interest. You may recall, I previously said banks are one of the most profitable businesses in the world because they leverage your money. If they pay you 1% to borrow your money, they can lend that money to someone else. If the bank earns 4% by lending it, they make a 300% ROI. The 1% the bank pays to control your money is their control cost.

The velocity of wealth is essentially how productive your dollar is or how much benefit your dollar can produce. The way to increase the velocity of your money is to increase its output while keeping its input constant. A collateralized loan is the best way to have your money working for you in two places at once. It can be gaining uninterrupted compounded interest and also be "used" for investment. With all this in mind, there are three elements involved in any controlled compounding situation:

1. Your money

You need to have your money saved in a place that is earning compounding interest, but it also needs to be where it has the ability to be leveraged (collateralized). I'm going to call this place you are holding your money, your "Master Account."

2. The entity you borrow money from

The entity needs to be willing to negotiate favorable terms for the loan and accept your money in your Master Account as dollar-for-dollar collateral. I'm going to call this your Lender.

3. What you want to purchase or invest in

The benefit you receive from what you purchase must be greater than the control cost that you pay the lender. If you pay 3% to the lender, you need to get a benefit greater than 3% in order for the deal to be profitable. If what you purchase is a liability (like a car), you have to value that purchase more than the control cost you pay.

The process of controlled compounding is fairly simple:

1. You place funds into your Master Account where your money will earn uninterrupted compound interest;

2. You identify what may be an asset or an activity that will produce a good ROR for you;

3. You approach the lender and determine the potential terms for a loan;

4. You use the lender's money in the form of a loan, leaving your money in your Master Account; and

5. Over time, you pay back the loan with amortized interest while collecting both the compounding interest in your Master Account, and if applicable, any investment gains.

Controlled compounding can be incredible if used for ROI positive activities like investing in assets or business endeavors. At the end of the investing process, your Master Account has grown, the loan has been paid off and you now have an additional asset working for you.

You have effectively "used" your money while continuing to receive uninterrupted compound interest.

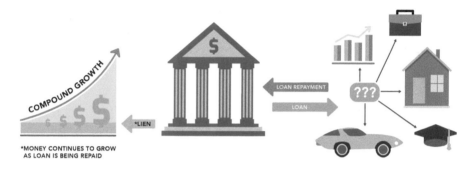

And you can do it again, and again and again. You're only limited by the amount of money you choose to put into it. An amount which is continuing to grow exponentially for the rest of your life.

9

Creating Your Master Account

As I set out in pursuit of a better way for my clients, I encountered a dizzying array of principles, opinions, products, strategies and tactics which seemed to make a lot of promises. They promised to protect money, grow money, generate a return, recoup a loss or guarantee success. I proceeded to uncover the fatal flaws in those which fell short of their claims and to identify the strengths of those which were able to fulfill theirs. And the simple truth is that there was a golden thread running through every strategy that delivered on its promises. It was efficient in doing whatever it was doing. It minimized a loss, maximized a gain or controlled something to improve it.

There was a corresponding consistency between those things that over-promised and under-delivered. They were inefficient in doing whatever it is they were doing. I could identify places that were losing money unknowingly or unnecessarily. I could define opportunities for gain that were being left on the table. I could see issues that, by applying a little control, could be adjusted and improved. There was no silver bullet. Instead, it was all about efficiency! It's not about any individual product: remember club vs. swing? It's about the necessary process in building wealth most efficiently.

The way you build wealth is by maximizing the efficiency of the whole process. The way you maximize the efficiency of the whole process is by maximizing the efficiency of each element of the process.

The Most Efficient Financial Vehicle

If you recall, the wealth equation ($E=mc^2$) helps you see that you need to have both a process and a financial vehicle that will provide your money with two things: uninterrupted compounding and unhindered control. Earlier, we reviewed the characteristics of an ideal account. The most efficient vehicle or product you entrust your money with should have as many of these characteristics as possible.

These characteristics include:

1. Safe

2. Liquid

3. Growth

4. Leverage

5. Inflation-Protection

6. Guarantees

7. Free of Fees

8. Free of Regulation

9. Flexible

10. Requires Minimal Time

11. Passive Cash Flow

12. Private

13. Protection

14. Tax-deductible

15. Tax-free Growth

16. Tax-free Distributions

The financial vehicle which comes as close to the ideal as possible is difficult to articulate clearly and something you can't readily search for on the Internet.

The very best place to setup your Master Account is with a mutual-owned life insurance company using a specially-designed, dividend-paying contract.

If I told you (before you ever picked up this book) that what you really need to add to your portfolio is life insurance, you probably would have thought I was, at best, mistaken, and at worst, trying to sell you something! You need to create wealth, reach your greatest potential and fund your **Why**. Everyone knows life insurance doesn't do that. Life insurance just provides for your family after you die.

Not so. Initially, life insurance had one main function, providing for dependents in the event of death. However, it also produced some positive effects including tax-free growth and tax-free access. Many of these effects ended up being a benefit to the insured while they were still living.

What mutual-owned companies and their contract-holders began to do was intentionally design their contracts to legally, and ethically, provide additional living benefits while maintaining the death benefits. They offered more ways for people to use their money during the accumulation and distribution phases while still providing for the legacy phase. It was important for the contract to keep the death benefits in place while remaining in the category of life insurance because it was the death benefit that made the living benefits possible.

A specially-designed, dividend-paying contract with a mutual-owned life insurance company is as close as you can get to an ideal financial vehicle.

It is the ultimate in efficiency. When I say it's the best, I mean it's the best by far. The runner-up (Roth IRA) is so far behind that it's no contest. The Roth IRA does deserve some attention. However, this chapter is devoted to discovering and describing the very best financial vehicle to use as your Master Account.

Let's take a more in-depth look at what the Master Account is and see how you can put it to work for you. There are five parts to the name (or description) of this financial vehicle.

1. Contract

First and foremost, it is a contract. A contract is an agreement between two parties. The contract governs the obligations and benefits of each party. This is important because your Master Account needs to be in a vehicle which serves you and, in which, you can trust.

Remember, the "known" is your friend while "unknowns" are your enemy. If you use a contract, you aren't going to put your money in a place where it is subject to the whims of the market or the needs of the government. You are going to place your money in a negotiated contract; a contract that is doubly advantageous to you.

The first of these contracts was written in the mid-1800s, expressly to manage wealth. This type of contract or agreement has evolved over time and is highly sophisticated and thoroughly vetted. What I mean is that it is complex and finely-tuned to satisfy the needs of both parties to a maximum degree. Eight generations of people like you and me, driven and determined to fund their **Why**, have negotiated, adjusted and augmented the terms of the contract. The result is an efficiently-designed agreement that serve both parties' interests.

Look at that date again. There is one important thing that did not exist in the mid-1800s – the federal tax code. This type of contract originated and developed in another time entirely. It germinated in the soil of private ownership. It does not share the deeply-ingrained assumption of our day that a portion of your funds are not yours.

The more you learn about this agreement, the more evident it becomes that it is designed with a deep respect for private ownership.

The assumption is that your money is your money and rightly should serve your interests.

Because these contracts predate the tax code, they fall securely under contract law, rather than tax law.

Changes to tax law, which shift tax thresholds and tax rates, simply do not apply to the money governed by this contract. Incredible, isn't it? Once you place your money in this contractual environment, it grows tax-free and can be accessed tax-free. And that is only one of the distinctive advantages of this type of contract.

2. Life Insurance Company

The party you enter into a contractual agreement with is a life insurance company. You would have to look far and wide to find a better financial partner. Life insurance companies are among the oldest and most stable institutions ever envisioned or created. In fact, the average age of these companies is over a hundred years. The consistent profitability they have shown, both for themselves and for their partners, is awe-inspiring. Consider this, life insurance companies have operated profitably and paid their contract-holders through the Civil War, both World Wars, The Great Depression and numerous recessions, including our most recent one – The Great Recession.

If you take a closer look at just one of those periods (The Great Depression of 1929-1938) you can get a feel for the depth and breadth of their stability and success. Throughout the economic boom of The Roaring 20s, people from all walks of life got caught up in something of a stock market fever and were pouring money into it. The stock market seemed to be such a sure bet that businesses and individuals alike were borrowing money and adding it to their brokerage accounts. Over a period of just a few days, in 1929, the stock market plummeted. The Dow Jones Industrial Average lost 90% of its value. The savings of millions of Americans from all segments of society were wiped out. Businesses and individuals who borrowed to finance their stock market fever went bankrupt, further exacerbating the economic toll. More than 9,000 banks became insolvent and shut their doors. A quarter of the population lost their jobs and was unable to find work as businesses continued to fail. It seemed that nobody escaped the ravages of the economic turmoil.

The exceptions in this dire scenario were life insurance companies and those who were in a contractual agreement with them. Throughout those years of turbulence, these quiet, durable companies remained virtually unscathed. Only about 2% of their assets were hindered in any way, and their contractual partners didn't lose a dime. On the contrary, they were paid the profits owed to them, according to the terms of the agreement, every year like clockwork.

It is a given that you should only do business with companies that have the greatest longevity, safety and profitability. You want a proven partner. That significantly narrows the pool of candidates.

Next, let's further define the particular kind of life insurance company with whom you will want to partner.

3. Mutual-Owned

When people come into my office, one of the first things they see is a framed stock certificate on the wall. By virtue of that certificate, I am a part-owner of the Green Bay Packers. You've got to understand the significance of this. Packers football is like a second religion in Wisconsin. Every game is sold out to season-ticket holders. On Sundays, the streets are totally empty because everyone is just fanatically into football. Even though I generally don't watch TV, I do make an exception to watch the Packers. Here's something you may not know about the Packers. They are the only NFL team that does not have a private owner; they're owned by the people.

The small cluster of select life insurance companies ideal for your Master Account are similarly unique. They are "mutual-owned." A mutual company is a private entity that is owned by its clients or contract-holders. The defining feature of a mutual company is that, since its customers are also its owners, they're first in line to receive any profits or income the mutual company generates.

I said earlier that your negotiated contract was going to be "doubly advantageous to you." I meant that quite literally. There are two parties within the contract, you and the life insurance company. But, because the life insurance company is mutual-owned, you actually have a vested interest in both parties. You are, at one and the same time, the contract-holder and a company owner. You are at a double advantage because you sit on both sides of the negotiation table. You can ensure that the contract maximizes the benefits to you and delight in the knowledge that a portion of any benefits the company receives will make its way into your pocket as well. Talk about a win/win situation!

The alternative to being a mutual company is being a stock company. Life insurance companies that are not mutual-owned are owned by their stockholders. They issue stock and trade in the market like any other public company. Stockholder-owned companies have the best interests of their stockholders firmly located before the best interest of their contract-holders. Their operations and bottom line are to serve the needs of the stockholders.

Mutual companies, however, have undivided and unconflicted interests. They serve the needs of one, and only one group of people, the contract-holders.

4. Dividend-Paying

Of all the strong, stable insurance companies out there, only a portion of them are mutual-owned. Of those mutual companies, only a segment of them offer generous dividend-paying contracts. It is these exclusive few that you want to select from in choosing your Master Account partner.

I just explained that a mutual-owned company has an obligation to pass on any profits it generates to its contract-holders. There are several ways a company can pay their contract-holders, and all of those ways are not created equal. The three primary ways this can be done are through dividends, interest or market-based products. Of those three options, dividends are the most preferable.

Let me explain why. Another word for dividend-paying is "participating." Dividends are a way to, "participate in the profits of a business." I've already shown that historically, life insurance companies have proven their ability to be reliably profitable. When you have a dividend-paying contract that allows you to participate in their profits, your profit potential is tied to the profit potential of the company.

However, if someone contracts to receive profits via interest or a market-based product, their profit potential is tied to the interest rate or the stock market. It's no contest. A dividend-paying contract will work harder and smarter for you over its lifetime than any comparable interest-bearing or market-based contract.

5. Specially-Designed

This is where it gets particularly exciting. The way you are going to design your contract is brilliant! What the design will do is maximize, and I do mean maximize, the number of, and the extent of, the benefits you can squeeze out of a dividend-paying contract with a life insurance company. The special design you are going to use will optimize the efficiency of the contract and the company, so your interests are served to the utmost degree.

The fundamental structure of a life insurance contract is that the contract-holder agrees to pay a certain amount of money. In return, the life insurance company agrees to pay out a certain amount of money when the contract-holder dies. If someone buys life insurance, they want to pay as little money as possible in order to receive as large a death payout as possible. When they do this, they get a whole lot of death benefit, and as I mentioned before, a relatively small amount of living benefits. That's what someone would do if they were just buying life insurance. But, that's not what you are doing. You're doing the exact opposite.

You want to design a contract in which you put in as much money as you can afford and get as little insurance as you have to in the process. In this way, you maximize the living benefits and minimize the death benefit.

MAXIMUM $$$$

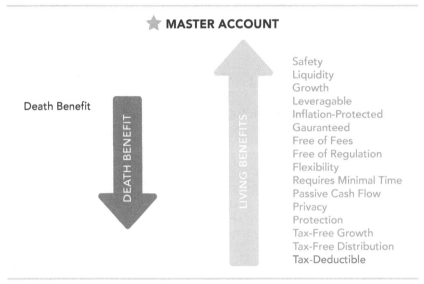

⭐ **MASTER ACCOUNT**

Death Benefit

DEATH BENEFIT

LIVING BENEFITS

Safety
Liquidity
Growth
Leveragable
Inflation-Protected
Gauranteed
Free of Fees
Free of Regulation
Flexibility
Requires Minimal Time
Passive Cash Flow
Privacy
Protection
Tax-Free Growth
Tax-Free Distribution
Tax-Deductible

MINIMUM $

Yes, I know it's counter-intuitive. It takes a bit to wrap your head around. Sometimes, people call this life insurance design "overfunded" or "max-funded." It might feel like you are buying really expensive insurance. In fact, that's what many uninformed critics will tell you. They'll say you are paying way too much for insurance. But, you are not.

You are buying a little bit of insurance and putting as much of your money as you can into a financial vehicle that you have optimized. You've created an account inside your insurance contract that is as close to ideal as you can possibly get.

You've created your Master Account:

- Any money you contribute beyond the cost of insurance is safe, liquid and is guaranteed to grow.

- It is growing even more as you receive dividends and can be used as collateral for a loan.

- There are no percentage-based fees, and you have flexibility in how you add funds to it.

89

- The contract provides some inflation protection and is fairly free from regulation.

- It requires very little time to manage and can be a source of passive cash flow.

- It grows tax-free and can be accessed tax-free.

- It can be protected from creditors and the death benefit provides protection for your family in the event of a tragedy. This is ultimately the best way to pass on your assets.

Do you recognize this list? It's the list of most of the characteristics of an "ideal account." When properly designed, your Master Account minimizes the death benefit and maximizes the living benefits. You can get everything in the "ideal account" other than tax-deductible contributions. A specially-designed, dividend-paying contract with a mutual-owned life insurance company is, categorically, the best and most efficient place to have your money.

The U.S. Government seems to think it's a pretty effective financial vehicle, too. For something like a hundred years, the wealthy and well-connected were happily using their contracts to grow and multiply their wealth. Money will always seek out places where it is treated well, and it was poured into these "accounts" by the millions. The number of people, businesses and banks who were making use of these Master Accounts grew and grew until they inevitably attracted the attention of the U.S. Government.

In 1988, the government moved to close what they saw as a tax loophole. Whereas previously, there were no regulations on the amount of money someone could put into an insurance contract, a guideline was put in place. It was decided that there was only a certain amount of insurance people could justify needing. If anyone put more money into their insurance contract, they needed to actually buy more insurance. If they didn't, the whole thing ceased to be classified as insurance and became something else. Conveniently, for the government, the "something else" was taxable.

Designing with the Guidelines in Mind

Recall again, when I talked about known and unknown? Once they know what the rules are, smart people and savvy business owners can turn a regulation into an advantage.

When designing your contract, you want to use the 1988 guidelines to your advantage. Conceptually, you want to maximize the living benefits early in your life (providing you the biggest impact) and die with the maximum amount of death benefits (ensuring that people you love and the things you want to accomplish are amply provided for). When designing and managing your contract, this is probably the most complex and technical issue you will want to watch carefully. Optimizing is all about getting the greatest, fullest and most complete mix of benefits possible. There are literally an infinite number of ways to structure your contract so that the mix of living and death benefits is optimized for you.

"Specially designed" means a whole lot of things but here is a quick summary:

The goal is to design a life insurance contract that will accept the largest amount of money you can manage to contribute and buy the smallest amount of insurance for which you qualify. Doing this will maximize the number and extent of the benefits you can squeeze out of it. Using the 1988 guidelines, various elements are tweaked to optimally provide for your life while preparing for your death.

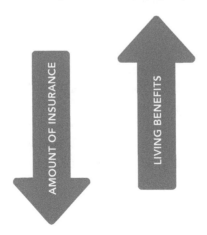

And there you have it. If done properly, you've created an account which is as close to the ideal as is possible. You have your Master

Account. The only financial vehicle you can use to gain control over your financial life today and maximize your future wealth potential.

Where This Strategy is Known

The wealthy and well-connected have known about these specially-designed contracts and special life insurance companies for decades. Many prominent individuals and corporations have taken advantage of these strategies.

- Walt Disney used money from his contract to finance the opening of Disney World.

- J. C. Penney tapped into the massive reserves he had accumulated in his contract in order to keep his company afloat through the Great Depression.

- When Ray Kroc bought McDonald's, he used his contract to pay his employees and create the successful Ronald McDonald marketing campaign.

- You might be surprised to know that every major bank uses this strategy to one degree or another. Bank of America holds roughly $19 billion of its assets in these types of contracts.

Where This Strategy is Unknown

Despite the fact that it's a common practice and recognized staple of banks, corporations and the wealthy, this strategy is relatively unheard of by people on the street. The next time you visit with someone who is connected with the insurance industry, or a financial investment advisor, ask them if they can explain how a specially-designed, dividend-paying contract with a mutual-owned life insurance company works. Don't ask them if they've ever heard about it or what they think about it. Ask them to explain how it works.

As a result of reading this book, you probably already understand it better than they do. If they bluster and bluff, you'll know it. And, if they say that somebody is just trying to sell you an insurance product that they can make an inflated commission on, you'll know for a fact that they don't know what they are talking about.

Why? One of the efficiencies inherent in these contracts relates to commissions. Remember, both parties, the contract-holder and the insurance company, are laser-focused on making this work in their favor. This contract is a golden goose for you and for the company, not for its agents. It is in the interest of the insurance company to keep their costs low. And, one of the ways that is done is by paying low commissions to their agents. The contract works in such a way as to ensure that the greater amount of living benefits provided, the lower the commission will be.

That's actually another reason why people haven't heard of it. There is little incentive for anyone to sell it to you.

I cut my financial teeth on a belief that life insurance was the absolute worst place to put money. Period. End of story. This idea was drilled into me early on, and it created the blind-spot that caused me so much grief. Even thinking about putting my client's money into life insurance made me grimace. Some of that response was certainly warranted. When life insurance isn't specially-designed, it's pretty terrible in the efficiency department. It puts a lot of unnecessary drag on your money. When I heard life insurance, I thought all of it was bad. It didn't occur to me that there was any difference between life insurance companies or that there's an infinite number of ways a contract can be written.

For instance, a typical life insurance contract is going to provide absolutely no liquidity in the early years. However, the contract I'm advocating can be designed in a way to give you early liquidity, even in the first year in most cases. That is radically different then 99% of the contracts that are being sold. I had to think long and hard about going on record as claiming that life insurance, in any form, is the best place for people to put their money. But, way back when I started this journey, I decided I was going to find a better way. I was going to do everything in my power to help as many people as possible see and reach their highest potential by showing them that better way.

I never thought that I would discover that the better way was utilizing life insurance.

10

Controlled Compounding Strategy™

Let's face it. I'm tired of writing out "specially-designed, dividend-paying contract with a mutual-owned life insurance company" every time I want to refer to that vehicle. And, you're just skipping over the words, anyway. So, for the remaining chapters, I'm just going to use the term "Master Account." Whenever I use the term "Master Account," I am referring to the most ideal financial vehicle which I've devoted a lot of time to describe to you.

You certainly can try to use a savings account, or, more appropriately, a properly-designed Roth IRA as your Master Account. But, it won't perform as well. That would be like perfecting your golf swing while using an inferior club. Both a savings account and a Roth IRA have their good points, for sure. They could work, but they're inefficient. Hopefully, by now, you share at least a portion of my passion for efficiency. From this point on, I'm going to assume your Master Account is going to be utilizing the preferred product. You have your eye on your **Why** and you have your Master Account which is the ultimate wealth building tool. Now you need to know how to use it.

Controlled Compounding – With Your Master Account

You're already aware that there are two things you want to do with your money.

1. Use uninterrupted compounding to enable it to grow exponentially.

2. Exercise unhindered control over it to cause it to grow explosively.

You want to have it all, the best of both worlds. Now, you are going to learn how to use a strategy that I call *Controlled Compounding*.

How to "Compound"

This "how to" is pretty simple. All you have to do is put as much money as possible into your Master Account. The account will do the rest. Every dollar you put into your account according to the terms of the contract will faithfully earn a competitive rate of compound interest for the rest of your life. Uninterrupted compounding is a passive strategy. You don't have to do anything to get it to work. While you don't have to do anything to get the benefit of uninterrupted compounding, there is one thing you can do to maximize it. Make a constant, conscious effort to discover and eliminate inefficiencies you find in any part of your financial life. Wherever you can minimize a loss or maximize a gain, take all of the money you free up and put it into your Master Account.

Remember when I showed you the difference between trying to get a greater return on your savings and freeing up more money (by being more efficient) to add to your savings? When you compare getting a greater return to having a greater amount of savings, adding more money to your savings is undoubtedly the better way. This is a paradigm shift that starts in the mind and works itself out in practice.

Make it a habit to think this way. Develop an efficiency mindset and savings discipline.

Your Master Account is going to work day and night for the rest of your life to compound your savings. Take your role in this seriously. Make sure it has a maximum amount of raw material (money) to work with. Think like a banker. Remember the principle of getting your money to flow to and through the bank before it gets to you.

Banks make money off your money before you use it. This is what you want to do as well. When you set up your Master Account, set it up so that as much money goes into the account to be saved and compounded as possible. But, in addition to your savings, put as much money as you are going to use (money for major purchases and investment) into it too. All of that money will be available to use (via a collateralized loan), but it will also compound, without interruption for the rest of your life.

To maximize the velocity of your money, get as much of it to flow to your Master Account as possible.

You don't have to do anything further. If for any number of reasons, you only want to exercise the passive compounding capability of your Master Account, that's your prerogative. However, if you want to engage in an active investment strategy, the Master Account is the only account out there that lets your money continue to earn compound interest without any interruptions for the rest of your life. Let me show you how controlled compounding is done.

How to Control

You can technically access money in your Master Account in one of two ways:

1. Since you have complete control over your policy, you can withdraw money straight out of your contract. The problem with this is once you withdraw a dollar, that dollar stops compounding. You lose that dollar and what it could have earned you over your lifetime. Efficiency requires that you say "no thanks" to exercising that option in your contract. The better way to access money in your Master Account is through a collateralized loan.

2. Remember when I explained leverage and collateral? You don't borrow your own money. You leave your money compounding in the account. Instead, you borrow from the life insurance company and use the money in your Master Account as collateral. The loans that you take don't have to go through underwriting (that cumbersome

process of proving to the lender that you deserve and can afford a loan). You don't have to prove that you need it or that you can repay it. You are pre-approved. You submit a simple request for a loan that adheres to the terms of your contract. Then, you receive a check in the mail from the life insurance company. Access to your funds will be quicker if your contract includes direct deposit.

The loan that you take is "non-structured." The life insurance company does not require you to pay this loan back by any particular time or in any particular amounts. It is called "non-structured" because there is no "structure" to the repayment. You can pay it back right away, in equal amounts over time, in lump sums whenever you have extra money or never pay it back at all. You can structure the repayment in whatever way benefits you most. Are you surprised that you can get a favorably negotiated, pre-approved, non-structured loan by using your Master Account?

This is only one of the numerous ways in which your Master Account is going to under promise and over deliver. As you head out on your financial journey with a Master Account in your portfolio, you're going to find yourself having this pleasantly-surprised feeling fairly often. The comments that you don't have to qualify for a loan and you can pay it back however you want may immediately cause some suspicion. I'm not selling something, and I'm not shading the truth. You don't have to take my word for it. It's all spelled out in the contract that creates your Master Account.

When you open your Master Account, it should be designed to include a "guaranteed loan provision." What this means is that the life insurance company guarantees it will lend to its contract-holders first before it invests that money anywhere else. The company is going to be taking the money you contribute to your Master Account and invest it profitably. It just makes sense that your mutual-owned life insurance company would let its contract-holders cut to the front of the lending line. That's why you're pre-approved and don't need to justify why you need the money or that you can afford to pay it back.

Imagine if your bank would give you (an account holder with them) a collateralized loan with the most favorable terms and allow you to pay it back in whatever way was most advantageous to you. Your bank won't do that, but your Master Account partner will!

Remember that life insurance companies have been profitable through any number of sticky economic situations for a couple of centuries now. Actuaries have finely-tuned algorithms in place and know with a high degree of certainty what their income and expenses are going to be. The life insurance company knows how to make a profit. The amount of interest they need to charge you on your collateralized loan is completely adequate for them to realize that profit. The way in which you pay it back is also completely adequate for them because they are playing a long-term game.

You can see that they can realize their profit if you pay the loan back ASAP, in regular payments or in lump sums. What if you don't pay it back at all? How can they offer you a loan that you never pay back? The answer is, again, in your contract.

Technically, there are three ways that a policy loan and accrued interest can be paid back:

1. Surrender

At any time during your life, you can surrender your contract. When you do, you essentially cancel the contract, "surrender" the death benefit and walk away with any money (over and above what you paid for your death benefit) in cash. This is also called "cashing out" your contract. You release the life insurance company from their obligation to pay anything to your beneficiaries at your death. The insurance company returns the "cash value" to you that is in your contract at the time you surrender it.

The problem with this is that once you surrender your contract, your money stops compounding. You lose those potential dollars and what they could have earned over your lifetime. You also lose all of the benefits of collateralized loans and all the other as close to ideal as possible benefits that your Master Account is providing. Efficiency requires that you say, "no thanks" to surrendering your contract. The better way to access money in your Master Account is through a policy loan.

2. Unstructured-Payments

The most likely way to repay the loan is through some form of payment. The life insurance company is playing the long-term game and doesn't care whether you pay right away (in which case, they will turn around and invest the repayment in another profitable way) or take a long time (in which case, they are earning the return they know they need in order to be profitable).

3. Death

If you never pay back the loan, then, according to the terms of your contract, your Master Account death benefit will pay off the portion that was collateralized and any accrued interest back to the insurance company. The remainder of the death benefit will be paid out to your beneficiaries tax-free. Remember that your Master Account has two kinds of benefits: death benefits and living benefits. Your death benefit will be reduced by the outstanding loan at the time of your passing.

When you practice controlled compounding by using a collateralized, non-structured loan provision, you are in control. You can make this loan work for you in whatever way is most profitable.

CONTROLLED COMPOUNDING WITH YOUR MASTER ACCOUNT

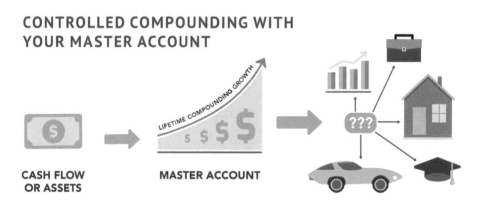

What If You Would Like to Access Your Money?

Right Away

Let's say you're made aware of an unexpected investment opportunity that you can't pass up. Getting a loan from a traditional lender would take too long. In this situation, you could take out a collateralized loan from your Master Account. Doing so gives you the ability to take advantage of the investment opportunity that you otherwise may have missed.

Equal Amounts Over Time

Let's say you need to buy a vehicle. You take out a collateralized loan from your Master Account, buy the vehicle outright, and then, make budgeted principal and interest payments back to the insurance company until the loan is repaid. There are three big advantages to this:

- First, by paying cash, you may be able to negotiate a lower price with the seller.

- Second, the money that you were loaned is still earning compound interest in your Master Account. You achieved the benefit of paying with cash. You also avoided the opportunity cost of paying cash from a different account. Now, that's efficiency!

- Third, you are paying interest back to the life insurance company rather than a credit card company or bank. You participate in the profits of the company via dividends so the interest you are paying contributes to the dividends that will eventually be added to your Master Account.

Using your Master Account this way is a more efficient way to purchase a vehicle. It leaves more money in your pocket. Remember, the definition of "asset" is something that makes you money. You have gained a greater level of mastery over how you spend your money, and your Master Account enabled you to do it.

Periodic Lump Sums

Let's say you want to flip houses. You take out a collateralized loan from your Master Account to cover the costs of putting a house under contract and to make the necessary repairs. Once the house is repaired and sold, you can take a portion of your proceeds to pay back part of the loan. By doing that, you're keeping a portion of your profits to purchase or repair your next house, if you desire. Otherwise, you can pay back the loan in its entirety, especially if it will be awhile before you purchase your next house.

Your Master Account has functioned as an asset and as a source of capital. Instead of being tied to bank loans (which you have to qualify for), you were your own source of financing. If credit dries up for everyone else, you can work all of the elements of the financing to your advantage. You were playing your own game.

Delay Repaying

I personally intend to use my Master Account in this way and hope that you consider taking advantage of the opportunity to do so as well. But, I've got to provide a disclaimer before I recommend this option. The wisdom of not repaying your loan depends on the efficiency of the whole system. You must be thoroughly aware of the particulars of your contract. You should not enter into this type of situation until you have some experience and a pretty thorough understanding of how your Master Account works. The scenario I am about to describe is one in which everything else being equal, someone might confidently choose to delay or never repay their loan.

Let's say you are considering an alternative investment which will produce a 13% return and offers the option to reinvest the returns year-by-year (your investment will compound). You take out a collateralized loan from your Master Account and put it into this investment. According to the terms of your contract, the rate on your loan from the insurance company is 5%.

Because you are getting a significantly better return on the alternative investment (13% compounded) than you are paying on your loan from the insurance company (5% compounded), you might well choose not to repay the loan. It is costing you 5% to earn 13% so you are effectively making 8%. But, remember that your ROI is actually 160%!

If you are wondering why the ROI is so high, go back and reread the chapter on "Controlling Your Money Like A Banker."

The oversight that can cause problems with not repaying the loan is related to the power of compounding. You need to remember that the 5% interest you are choosing not to pay on the loan is compounding. If someone borrowed 5% to make 13%, but they did not reinvest the profits, the compounding interest they are paying on the loan could outgrow the simple interest they are making on the investment. In some cases, a contract could be overleveraged causing you to lose your Master Account. Unfortunately, it's a common error and a very costly way to learn a lesson.

Please consult with someone who has experience doing this before proceeding on your own.

11

The Only "And Asset"

The Master Account is the only financial vehicle available today that allows your money to grow AND be used at the same time.

The **AND** Asset enables you to earn uninterrupted compound interest for the rest of your life **and** utilize your capital for other things. You can earn compound interest **and** buy your vehicles, **and** buy real estate, **and** trade stocks, **and** invest in private placements, **and** start a business, **and** engage in any profitable activity that you can dream of!

I was 19 years old when I started my first life insurance contract. While I didn't know as much as I do now, I knew enough to pull the trigger and get started. I set up a Master Account and started funding it with $400 a month. That was a bit of a stretch for me, but I knew it would be worth it long-term. Even now, just three years later, it's paying off handsomely.

Knowing what I know now, I would have designed the contract differently and gone with a different company, but I do not regret the decision to get started. What intrigued me the most was that I could save more money, have it grow for the rest of my life and could use it however I saw fit.

When it Makes Sense

I've said that you can take a collateralized loan for whatever reason you want. So how do you know when it makes sense to do so? I'll answer this by showing you an efficient retirement plan and two personal examples of what I did with my first collateralized loans.

Retirement Income and Legacy Planning

Taking a policy loan for retirement can be a very powerful way to obtain income for several reasons. Utilizing a policy loan will provide you with tax-free income. Your dividends will be growing at an exponential rate due to the power of compound interest. Because of this, you can receive more than the typically-cited industry-standard withdrawal rate of 3%.

Since your policy loan is collateralized, you're not spending down your assets like a traditional retirement account. This could allow you to receive income for a longer period of time. Legacy planning is an important piece of every financial plan. Life insurance is the most efficient way to pass on your legacy to the next generation. This legacy will be passed on tax-free.

You Can Make Money

Whenever you can make money, it makes sense to take a policy loan. This is when you have access to an opportunity outside of your Master Account that is ROI positive. If the return on the money you are taking out for the loan is greater than the cost of the loan itself, the loan is efficient and makes sense.

It makes sense to take a 5% loan out if you use it to make 5% or more in returns. With one of my first collateralized loans, I started my business. Any business has a number of startup and ongoing costs which can be pretty significant until they begin to be covered by cash flow. I borrowed those startup costs, as well as the costs of publishing this book, from the life insurance company that holds my contract.

This loan is ROI positive. The long-term profit that results from the initial funding of my business has already been significant and is likely to only grow over time. The dollars in my Master Account are going to continue to grow into the future whether my business is successful or a complete failure. What's special is that I've leveraged them in order to launch and grow my business today.

You Can Make a Difference

Taking a policy loan also makes sense if it provides you the opportunity to significantly contribute to your *Why*. Within the first year of funding my policy, I had an opportunity to go to Guatemala for a week-long service project. I don't want to wait until my retirement years to volunteer, give back and do good in the world. I want to leave a legacy today! One of my personal goals is to serve the underprivileged somewhere outside of the U.S. every year. So, I borrowed the money to fund the trip from my Master Account and set up a structured repayment plan. Granted, this did mean that I paid interest on the amount I had borrowed. It technically cost me more to serve than the cost of the trip. But, I'm willing to pay amortized interest (on my loan) in order to earn compound interest (on the money in my Master Account) for all the reasons I've given in the preceding chapters.

I remember sitting on the airplane thinking how surreal it felt that the money in my Master Account was continuing to grow, but because of controlled compounding, I could be in Guatemala, serving at the same time. Using a collateralized loan to serve in Guatemala was not an ROI positive decision on my personal wealth balance sheet. However, I put a greater value than the control cost (the amount of interest I paid on the loan) on using those funds to serve in Guatemala. It was worth every penny.

There are innumerable different reasons you might use a collateralized loan. The ways I used mine are examples of collateralized loans anyone can use to their advantage. Whether you fund your contract with $400 a month or $400,000 a month, the principles stay the same. Your money compounds without interruption at the same time that you can leverage it for your benefit. The concepts you have learned can be applied by individuals and to various financial scenarios alike. A few examples are listed below:

Entrepreneur - As an entrepreneur, you are your greatest asset and your business is your greatest investment. Using what you have learned, you can save for the future and invest your capital into your business or other entrepreneurial endeavors at the same time.

Investor - Investing (in some fashion) has almost become second-nature in our society. You now know how to invest in opportunities using the most efficient process available.

High Income - Having a high income generally means you're going to pay a lot of money in taxes. You now know how to save more money, have tax-free income and pass on your wealth in the most efficient manner.

Inexperienced - Beginning to save or invest can be a daunting challenge. Knowing how to master your money and minimize wealth transfers will put you in a fantastic, wealth-building position.

Experienced - Even the savviest money managers should constantly be learning. Leveraging your current knowledge with the concepts you have learned will further enhance your wealth success.

Retirement - The three massive benefits of the Master Account to a retiree are safety, tax-free income and guaranteed growth. This maximizes the income you will be able to receive without the fear of having to go back to work following a market crash.

Family - In its most basic form, the Controlled Compounding Strategy™ is a forced savings plan. Families are willing to save more money if they know they can have access to that money for vacations, buying cars or preparing for college.

College Planning - Unlike other college planning financial vehicles, you won't get penalized if you decide not to go to school. You can use your Master Account for various other things like buying a car, wedding planning, house down payment and even a retirement supplement plan.

Debt - Many of you reading this book have debt. Some have a lot of debt. Using the Controlled Compounding Strategy™, you can start saving today and get lifetime compound interest. Then use those savings to pay off your debt.

At the end of chapter five, I discussed the ROI of a golf club. I love using this example because I believe I have given you the very best golf club (ideal financial vehicle). Now, you also have an idea of how to perfect your swing (using the concepts of the Controlled Compounding Strategy™). Saving your money in a tax-free manner while having access to capital is a tremendous asset. Cash is king. Now, you know how to save more of it and have access to it.

Ultimately, it comes down to what I stated in the introduction of this book. You are your number one asset. Use your money in a way that backs up that statement.

12

Summing It All Up

Let's review the key concepts that I have shared with you in this book. You are your own greatest asset! Your ability to think and then act is one of the greatest qualities you have as a human being. You also have another great asset that can work for you – time. Your ability to think and act in a strategic manner can lead to tremendous wealth accumulation over time. Whatever your age and stage in life, you can make solid progress toward building a passive income stream that will finance your life and your *Why* at a level beyond what you currently may think is possible.

Whatever your current financial plan is, you are likely losing money unknowingly or unnecessarily. Finding those losses and putting an end to them is crucial to maximizing the efficiency of your wealth plan. The significant financial expenses you have may include buying homes, paying taxes, fees, education, investing and major purchases (like vacations, cars, etc.). Wealth transfers can happen during any of these transactions and without you knowing. Any time a wealth transfer occurs, you lose more than you think. As you have learned, wealth transfers cost you significantly more than just the initial loss. When you lose a dollar, you don't just lose that dollar, but you also lose the opportunity of what that dollar could have earned you over your lifetime. Opportunity costs are a fundamental truth about money. They are the loss of potential gain from other alternatives when one alternative is chosen. All of your decisions have secondary effects, either positive or negative.

Efficiency, the "E" in E=mc^2, will only make whatever you are doing, better. It will make it better through all the stages of your life. Whether you are an entrepreneur, investor, employee or retiree, maximizing the efficiency of your financial strategy from beginning to end is sure to enhance whatever you are doing.

Compounding, if left alone to work its magic over time, will always produce an exponential yield. Albert Einstein has been credited over the years in various financial publications as stating: "Compound interest is the eighth wonder of the world." Another statement often attributed to him declares: "He who understands it, earns it. He who doesn't, pays it."

Control might be the ninth wonder of the world, but it's nothing special if you don't learn how to master it and use it for your benefit. A banker's goal is to take every dollar that comes through their door and squeeze as many benefits out of that dollar as possible. While you can't use other people's money to the extent that banks do, you can use it more effectively than you may think. You can also adopt some of their best practices and create your own system for controlling money.

Controlled compounding can be incredible if used for ROI positive activities like investing in assets or business endeavors. At the end of the investing process, your Master Account has grown, the loan has been paid off and you now have an additional asset working for you.

When properly designed so that it minimizes the death benefit and maximizes the living benefits, your Master Account can get everything associated with the "ideal account" except for tax-deductible contributions.

Your Master Account is an **AND** Asset. It enables you to earn uninterrupted compound interest for the rest of your life **and** utilize your capital for other things. You can earn uninterrupted compound interest **and** buy your vehicles, **and** buy real estate, **and** trade stocks, **and** invest in private placements, **and** start a business, **and** engage in any profitable activity that you can dream of!

For more information, visit us at
www.betterwealthsolutions.com or contact us at
info@betterwealthsolutions.com!

Epilogue

What I live for is to see and reach my highest potential.
It's my personal mission to help as many people as possible
see and reach their highest potential.

The most meaningful word in my mission statement is the word "see." My life radically changed when I started seeing for myself the potential I never thought I had. If I could only do one thing through this book, it would be to show you how you can start "seeing." Grasping the money truths and the concepts involved in the wealth equation is essential to help you see and reach your highest potential.

It was only a few days after I first considered the idea of a book that I finished the earliest outline of it. It has gone through a lot of addition, deletion and revision since then, but it represents my very best effort at helping you to see and reach your highest potential. It is my attempt to show you a better way, financially.

I want you to know how excited I am that you have read all the way to the end. Not only because of what it says about you, but what it means for you. It says that you are diligent, inquisitive and an active learner. It means that you now have a working knowledge of the most powerful financial concepts and the most ideal product available today. I've done the work I need to do. Imperfectly, I'm sure, but as fully as I am able. I can only hope that it is of as much benefit to you as I intended it to be.

Thank you for coming along with me on my journey.
And thank you for the privilege of letting me be a part of yours.